Edwin Brickwood

Boat racing or the arts of rowing and training

Edwin Brickwood

Boat racing or the arts of rowing and training

ISBN/EAN: 9783742806758

Manufactured in Europe, USA, Canada, Australia, Japa

Cover: Foto ©Stingray / pixelio.de

Manufactured and distributed by brebook publishing software (www.brebook.com)

Edwin Brickwood

Boat racing or the arts of rowing and training

Dedication.

TO

GEORGE MORRISON, Esq.,

OF

BALLIOL COLLEGE, OXFORD,

THIS WORK IS INSCRIBED,

AS A TOKEN OF ESTEEM AND GRATITUDE,

BY HIS OBLIGED FRIEND,

THE AUTHOR.

PREFACE.

TEN years have elapsed since the republication, under the title of "The Arts of Rowing and Training," of a series of articles which, from time to time, appeared in the columns of the *Field* newspaper, and which, with several original chapters subsequently added, were designed to form a manual on boatracing. This manual, on its completion, was submitted to a gentleman who was not only an accomplished oarsman himself, but the most experienced coach of his day; and, having been revised by him before passing into the hands of the printer, embodied the precepts which, under his personal instruction, mainly contributed to the repeated successes of Oxford crews in the University Boat Race, and at a later period to the turn of the tide in favour of Cambridge. The principles enunciated in it were, consequently, not wanting in authority. As the book has long been out of print, and a new edition is called for, advantage has been taken of the present reissue to rewrite it, and to supplement it with such information as will render it more complete than hitherto, and bring it into harmony with modern usage—great changes, such as the invention of the sliding seat, the abolition of coxswains in four oars, and the practice of steering by means of the feet of one of the oarsmen rowing in a crew, having brought about a revolution in boat racing almost as complete as the supercession of the old-fashioned inrigged craft by the modern outrigger, upwards of thirty years ago.

An important alteration, too, has taken place in the conduct of boat races, for it was found that, owing to various causes, the original rules scarcely met the questions which, from time to time, arose in disputed races, and this was more especially the case in watermen's matches. An entirely new code of boatracing laws consequently became necessary, and were drawn up by a congress of boating men in 1872. The results of their deliberations—which, by the way, have been productive of much benefit—are given, with explanations in the proper place.

In regard to other points incidental to boat racing, in which my own experience as an arbiter has not been sufficient to dispel any doubts that may have arisen in my mind as to the best course to pursue, I have consulted an authority than whom none ranks higher —Mr. John Ireland, of the London Rowing Club, and for his valuable advice and assistance I must not fail to express my acknowledgments; as well as to the "Head of the Water" at St. Peter's College, for a perusal of the "Ledger" containing the early records of boating at Westminster.

From the works of Mr. McMichael on the "Oxford and Cambridge Boat-races;" Mr. Knollys on "Boating at Oxford; Mr. Blake-Humfrey on "Eton Boating;" "Stonehenge" on "British Rural Sports;" the Oxford pamphlet, the "Principles of Rowing and Steering;" the "American Oarsman's Manual," kindly presented to me by the author; Dr. Edward Smith on "Practical Dietary;" Mr. McClaren on "Training;" as well as several aquatic guide-books now out of print, I have occasionally borrowed in my text: and to Messrs. Barraud and Jerrard, of Gloucester-place, I am indebted for the excellent photograph of the Grand Challenge Cup, from which the vignette on the cover of this book has been engraved.

For imperfections in style, and for possible short-comings in the historical records, I must beg my readers' indulgence; but the difficulty of verifying the latter has been almost insurmountable. Still, if boating men are disposed to regard this work as an authority, in the future as in the past, I shall be amply rewarded for my labours.

E. D. B.

The Temple, London,
    March, 1876.

CONTENTS.

PART I.—ROWING.

CHAPTER		PAGE
I.	Introduction: Past and Present Condition of Boatracing	1
II.	Racing Boats: Their History and Fittings . . .	10
III.	The Sliding Seat: Its Invention, Adoption, and Theory	26
IV.	How to Use an Oar, and Sculls.	40
V.	Faults and Errors: What to avoid	59
VI.	Steering: Coxswain and Non-coxswain . .	66
VII.	Teaching Beginners.	78
VIII.	Coaching for Races, and Selection of Crews . .	88
IX.	The Varieties and Conduct of Boatraces. . . .	102
X.	The Laws of Boatracing	116
XI.	The Qualifications of Amateurs	128
XII.	Boat Clubs: Their Organisation and Administration	135
XIII.	Historical Records, A.D. 1715 to 1838	147
XIV.	,, ,, A.D. 1839 to 1855	163
XV.	,, ,, A.D. 1856 to 1875	177

b

CONTENTS.

PART II.—TRAINING.

CHAPTER		PAGE
XVI.	Its Principles	197
XVII.	Its Practice	206
XVIII.	Prohibitions, Ailments, &c.	221

APPENDIX.

Rules for Betting. 235

INDEX . . 277

THE ARTS

OF

ROWING AND TRAINING.

PART I.—ROWING.

CHAPTER I.

INTRODUCTORY REMARKS: PAST AND PRESENT CONDITION OF BOAT RACING.

BOATING is a sport which has long been popular with the youth of the day, and which grows in favour the more it is practised, and the better it is understood. Not only is it followed as a relaxation and an amusement, but it may almost be said to have become a part of the physical discipline which is now on all hands admitted to be not incompatible with, but positively conducive to, that mental and moral training, in view of the more serious business of life, which forms our national education. Field sports and athletic exercises, among which none is less objectionable than rowing, are now recognised not only as an integral part but a necessity of any sound system of instruction. *Mens sana* will be found in *corpore sano*. The author of "Tom Brown's School Days'"—himself an instance of combined muscular Christianity and intellectual development—has shown us that mind and muscle are not necessarily antagonistic, and that Tom Brown at Oxford was no lower in the class lists for being an accomplished athlete. Again, George Denman, now on the Bench, was not prevented from attaining the highest honours of the Classical Tripos by twice rowing in the Cambridge crew against the sister University. The battle of Waterloo was said by the Iron Duke to have been won on the playing fields of Eton. Hence the value of these exercises not only as a means to the enjoyment of health, but as aiding to form character and discipline the intellect. And in after life how essential it is for the maintenance of the necessary equilibrium, that the over-wrought brain should find some relaxation in the sports of the field, to enable it to return refreshed and renewed to take its part in the daily struggle for existence : and though in this case, recourse is not had to the racing boat, yet change of air and scene, bodily fatigue, and physical exertion, are yearly sought and undergone by the hardworked man of business, who departs for his shooting or fishing in the north, or for a cruise in his yacht in the Channel, with this end in view.

Rowing, as practised at the present day, combines more completely than any other open air sport the best features of physical training. Its prominent value as an exercise consists in its bringing into play a great number of muscles and bodily organs, thus imparting vigour to the whole frame; and since the art is acquired only by long continued and assiduous practice, it is the more susceptible of being influenced by a judicious system of bodily preparation and training. In comparing the relative merits of different kinds of sports as regards their effects on the mind as well as on the body, that one may be assumed to be the best which affords the most ample scope for the employment of the greatest number of the highest faculties; and which, while calling into play the full measure of muscular strength and physical endurance, still renders the body perfectly subordinate to, and a quickly responsive and willing instrument of, the mind. Tried by such a test, rowing stands exceptionally high, particularly when we consider it under the aspect of its use in racing; for where success has to be striven for in vigorous and excited competition, not only are strength and endurance needed, but also plenty of that high moral quality known as "pluck," and a correct and delicate appreciation of the best time and method of applying, utilizing to their utmost, and perfectly controlling, the forces employed. Modern improvements in racing boats have reduced the rowing of the present day to a finer art than ever, rendering it less than formerly the rude conflict of force it was in the early days of racing boats, when such contests were commonly mere exhibitions of uncultivated powers propelling heavy bulks by main strength.

Boat racing was not much in vogue until the latter part of the eighteenth, and the beginning of the present century—rowing until then having mainly been used for the conveyance of passengers and goods.

Of late, however, it has grown rapidly in popular estimation.

Twenty years ago there was not one regatta in England where now there are a score. Henley and the Thames National, it is true, held their own; there were the customary college races at the Universities, but there was little else which might be termed attractive: for, strange to say, the Oxford and Cambridge match had scarcely become an annual affair, and aroused comparatively little interest, as it was witnessed mainly by a few hundreds of rowing men, instead of by the tens, or it may be hundreds, of thousands of spectators who now throng the banks of the Thames when the Easter boat race is decided; and the Wingfield Sculls, the coveted trophy of amateur scullers, was too often nothing but a row over the course. Boat building was in its infancy; the instruction of oarsmen no less than the preparation of crews was an unwritten arbitrary pedantry; the trainer was an empiric; the umpire was fortunate if he knew where to find a copy of the rules of boat racing by which to be guided; the sporting journalist was scarcely invented; and the daily press knew not "stroke oars" and "coaches." All this is now changed. Town begins its season with the usual excitement about "dark blue" and "light blue." Putney is besieged for a fortnight before the University crews fight their annual battle between the Aqueduct and the Ship. The banks of the Thames are lined with unwonted carriages, occupied by scores of the upper classes, and society is more exercised about the result of a boat race than about the new budget or the rate of income tax. Henley opens the summer campaign with its unequalled tournament, to be followed by a mob of regattas, metropolitan and provincial. The rivers are covered as the season advances with hundreds of oarsmen and scullers in assiduous practice, and, when the autumn comes, an International match, be it in England or America, is by no means uncommon. Not only has the sport taken deep root in the Emerald Isle, where it is pursued with no measured success on the Liffey, the Shannon, and the Lee; but the waters of the United States and the Dominion of Canada have become the arena of regattas and inter-collegiate races by dozens, to say nothing of many a contest between the old and the new worlds. Australia, too, Hindostan, the Celestial Empire, and the Republics of South America, have witnessed the modern spectacle of an English boat race, and so have the great Continental cities of Paris, Hamburgh, St. Petersburgh, and Buda-Pesth, nearer home—so world-wide has the art become.

Sea rowing, too, has made rapid improvement during the last eight or ten years, salt-water crews having held their own more than creditably in competition, on the South Coast of England, with some of the best professional oarsmen of the River Thames; though it may be, occasionally, in boats and under conditions more or less unfavourable to the fresh water crews. Margate, Ramsgate, Hastings, St. Leonards, and Worthing, have all witnessed contests of this nature, to the no small benefit of local oarsmanship; and so has Brighton, where the number of crews and the quality of the rowing is marvellous, if the unfavourable and exposed condition of the beach and roadstead, with no harbour whatever, is taken into consideration. Farther west, too, on Southampton water, in the estuary of the Exe, at Teignmouth, in Dartmouth Harbour, and inside Plymouth breakwater, some really good rowing, on the part of the dwellers in those regions, as well as of the crews of more than one well known racing yacht, may be witnessed annually by the company attending the autumn gatherings of the South and West. And that good oarsmanship is not confined to the male sex alone, is attested by the number of ladies to be seen rowing an oar or a pair of sculls on the Thames, and will be vouched by anyone who has beheld the four-oared galley races between the fisherwomen of Saltash and Devonport, which form a most interesting feature of the West of England rowing regattas.

Strangely enough, notwithstanding this manifest increase in the popularity of amateur oarsmanship, professional rowing has not kept pace with it. On the contrary, it has declined in a marked manner, comparatively little interest being taken in watermen's matches, which, in the days of Coombes, Cole, the Mackinneys, Newell, Messenger, Kelley, and Chambers, created such vast excitement; while the modern Thames Regatta, which hovers over the ashes of the old time-honoured Thames National, brings but a limited company to Putney, and that none of the best. The case, however, is totally different on the Tyne, where a professional sculling match is the signal for little short of a general holiday, and where the enormous crowds which assemble on the Gateshead and Newcastle sides of the river would lead a foreigner to think some grand pageant or review was about to be held. Whether this decline of professional rowing—in so far as the metropolis, at any rate, is concerned—be attributable to dissensions among the watermen is open to question; but perhaps various causes, in themselves comparatively trifling, may, when added together, have contributed to bring about this result. And oddly enough, in proportion as the lower classes of the capital have forsaken the very matches which, of all others, would naturally interest them most, so have they taken to the University boat race, which, for obvious reasons, would be more likely to prove attractive to the middle and upper classes. To this state of things it is possible the International boat races of late years have to some extent conduced, commencing with the race in 1869 between representative four-oared crews of the Universities of Oxford in the mother country and Harvard in the United States of America; and ending with the match between the London Rowing Club and the Atalanta Boat Club of New York in 1872, both rowed on the Thames between Putney and Mortlake.

The standard of rowing is maintained by the Universities and Colleges of Oxford, Cambridge, and Dublin; by the public schools—Eton in particular—and by the principal boat and rowing clubs of the Thames and the provinces, such as the London, Leander, Kingston, Thames, Tyne, Chester, Lancaster, Kingstown, Cork, and many others too numerous to mention. Of course, club matches—in which generic term may be included college and other races at the

Universities—tend to uphold it; but without the competition at the great gathering of amateur oarsmen and scullers at Henley, and in a lesser degree between Oxford and Cambridge crews at Putney, it would scarcely be kept up at the height to which it reaches. That it should fluctuate from time to time is a necessity, and that in occasional years it is of an exceptionally good class is only natural, as likewise that in other years it falls to a comparatively low pitch. Speed has increased—of that there is no doubt; the displacement of the now obsolete boats with keels by the keelless single-streak cedar outriggers having tended to this end, while the mechanical gain afforded by the new sliding seat has assisted in its development. Form perhaps has not improved, but better things may be hoped for, as the use of the new tools becomes more familiar. The science of "coaching" is more fully known and more readily comprehended than in days gone by; and, when divested of the humbug and bewildering technicalities with which it has been needlessly surrounded, is found a far simpler task than it was believed to be. The art of "training" has been rescued from the depths of empiricism in which it was too long suffered to dwell, and in which the ignorant prejudices of illiterate professionals, who at one time usurped the coaching of amateurs, purposely kept it. At the present time it is conducted on the principles of common sense and hygiene, and so far from being involved in mystery is now nothing more nor less than an adhesion to a few simple rules of bathing, diet, exercise, and rest

INTRODUCTION.

The conduct of regattas, and the duties of committees, umpires, and judges, are now thoroughly well understood, and have over and over again been openly discussed and ventilated; and the written rules for their guidance, no less than the unwritten practice of their office, are from time to time amended, as the force of circumstances and the test of experience render necessary. This satisfactory state of things is mainly due to public opinion, as manifested through the press; for there can be no gainsaying the fact that to the sporting journals in particular, and more recently to the daily press in a limited degree, the boating world is indebted for the sweeping away of effete abuses, and the institution of a régime more in accordance with the requirements of the age.

CHAPTER II.

RACING BOATS: THEIR HISTORY AND FITTINGS.

THE boats used in racing, by means of the oar and scull, are for the most part outriggers. They comprise eight-oars, four-oars, pair-oars, and sculling-boats, and they have long superseded the old style, in which the rowlock was fixed upon the gunwale or wale streak. Six-oars are in general use in America, but they are not fashionable in England.

The term outrigger means something that is fitted or rigged out—*i.e.*, beyond the gunwale of a boat—and, properly speaking, applies to the iron framework rigged out from the side to support the rowlocks; but it is conventionally applied to the outrigged boats themselves, which, however incorrect it may be in strictness, are commonly called "outriggers"—thus an eight-oared outrigger, a pair-oared outrigger, &c. Before alluding to them more fully, it may not prove uninteresting to sketch a short history of the invention and general adoption of these iron rods, or outriggers proper, which enable the width of the boat to be reduced, and yet, by giving more leverage, permit longer and more powerful oars and sculls to be used than in old-fashioned or inrigged boats. The invention has been generally accredited to the late Henry Clasper, of Newcastle-on-Tyne; but the following information, derived from reliable and trustworthy authority,* explains the real facts of the case, and may be considered conclusive.

The first outriggers used in racing were fixed on a boat called the "Diamond," of Ouseburn, Tyneside, when she rowed against the "Fly," of Scotswood-on-Tyne, in the year 1828; but they were only rude pieces of wood fastened on the sides, and were invented by Anthony Brown, of Ouseburn, and fixed by Ridley, a boat-builder of that period. In the same year Frank Emmet claimed the invention, and fixed something similar on a boat belonging to Dent's Hole, Tyneside; and it is not disputed that the "Eagle," of Dent's Hole, by Emmet, in the year 1830, was the first boat with outriggers of iron. Outrigged craft then came to be the usual form of racing boats on the northern rivers, Tyne and Wear. Nevertheless, when regular regattas were established by the Durham University about 1834 or 1835, London-built six-oared racing boats were procured from Searle, but they were found to be so inferior in speed to the native outriggers, that the latter were not allowed to compete in the same races; and consequently the boats were divided for separate races into two classes, *i.e.*, cutters and gigs (as the outriggers were then termed.) The force of southern fashion, however, appears so far to have prevailed over common sense and experience—just as four-horse coaches for a long while prevailed over Stephenson's iron horse—that many boats of the London pattern were built in the north after that time, until

---

* Authentic Letters in *The Field*, of Jan. and Feb., 1865.

the Clasper victories on the Thames in 1844 and 1845 established the reputation of the northern type of boat. The principle of Clasper's boat was the same as the traditional form, but he was the first builder who reduced the substance of the boat to the limit of lightness and fine workmanship, or nearly so, as the racing outrigger has unquestionably undergone a marked improvement since he achieved his well-deserved reputation. In 1842, then, Clasper commenced to build the four-oared boat which was to produce such a revolution in the art of boat building in the south; but he was dissuaded from completing her for the 300*l*. match with Coombes's crew, which took place on the Tyne on the 16th July, 1842. In this match Clasper was defeated, and he attributed it to his old fashioned heavy boat. He subsequently completed his new four-oar, and appeared with her at the Thames National Regatta, at Putney, in 1844; where he succeeded in winning the 50*l*. prize on the 21st June, although he was defeated—perhaps owing to bad steerage—by Robert Coombes's crew in the champion race for the purse of 100*l*. on the following day. In the succeeding year, however, he won the chief prize for fours, in a boat built of mahogany, in several narrow streaks: she was called, it is said, the "Five Brothers," and her iron outriggers were only 8 inches long. At a subsequent period Clasper brought up to London a single-streak boat.

In 1838 a pair-oared outrigger, called the "Knife," was built in Dublin by a coach builder named Allpress, who constructed various kinds of boats. She was built in seven streaks on each side, and measured

32ft. 2in. in length, 2ft. 8in. from gunwale to gunwale (outside) at her widest part, and was fitted with iron outriggers each $7\frac{1}{4}$ inches long. A sculling outrigger also appears to have been built at Putney in the summer of 1844—the same year in which Clasper brought his novel boat up to London, but six months beforehand—by Samuel Wolsencroft, of that village, for Mr. Westropp, of the Civil Engineers College, which then stood on the spot whence the Cedars now overlook the Thames, below the bridge. She was a single plank boat, but as the skin was not bent before being fitted, she soon split, although when repaired she lasted some years. In the following year, 1845, a four-oared outrigger was built by W. Biffen, of Hammersmith, and was his first attempt at the new craft. In her his crew rowed for and won the Landsmen's prize at the Thames Regatta of that year.

The introduction of the outrigger now became general, but at first the new boats were built with keels; in course of time, however, they became more and more improved upon, and outward keels were discontinued. Outriggers were first used in the match between Oxford and Cambridge in 1846, and in 1857 the Universities met in the modern keel-less eights for the first time, using also round-loomed oars; while sliding seats were first used, and by both, in the Putney match of 1873. It must, however, be admitted that the boating world of the present day is mainly indebted to Harry Clasper for the cardinal improvements in the modern racing outrigged boat. At the hands of Clasper himself, and other builders, she has received those finishing touches which make her what she now is.

The modern single-streak race boat is composed, if it may be so said, of two parts, viz., the body or boat itself, and the outriggers or iron rods which carry the rowlocks. The body is usually built of cedar wood, in lengths, with ribs or "timbers" of ash (and occasionally of beech) fixed above in the inwale—a long strip of deal running lengthwise down the inside of the upper edge of the boat—and below in the inner keel or kelson.

Upon the inner keel is fastened a long piece of wood, generally fir, which rises in the centre, under the seats or thwarts which are fastened to it, to their level, and tapers off fore and aft; the object of this false kelson or backbone being to impart strength to the floor of the boat, and to assist in supporting the thwarts. These latter are now placed much lower in a boat than in the days of fixed seats, because they have to carry the upper or sliding seat which shifts backwards and forwards coincidently with the oarsman himself. They are also longer fore and aft than formerly, to the extent of several inches in front and astern, so as to afford as much play as 18in. to the shifting seat. On the top of the lower or stationary thwart are fixed two flat oblong brass rods, 18in. long by $\frac{1}{2}$in. wide and $\frac{1}{3}$in. deep, upon which boxwood or bone runners, fastened to the under part of the movable or sliding seat, work backwards and forwards in a line parallel to the kelson, in which movement they are aided by the application of grease. Stops fore and aft prevent the shifting seat from running off the rails or getting out of gear. The latest improvement consists in dispensing with the under or lower thwart, and in using instead of it two inverted wooden frames, about 16in. or 18in. in length, and 1½in. in width, and the same in depth, into which tubes for the runners to play upon are sunk. These frames run lengthwise down the boat, *i.e.*, parallel with the kelson, and being fixed on supports at either end obviate the necessity of a solid under-thwart, and so save wood and weight. Into these frames brass tubes in some cases, in others glass (Searle's patent), are sunk, but the former—and this is the case with all brass fittings for slides—soil the oarsmen's flannels badly, while glass slides are prone to break. The best and the newest are of zinc, upon which boxwood runners on the under part of the sliding seat play to and fro with the least possible friction, especially if occasionally lubricated with a little oil. This zinc tubing is nothing more nor less than hollow zinc piping. Boxwood seems better adapted for runners than bone.

The inner keel, kelson and inwale are first laid down, bottom upwards, on the frame upon which these boats are usually built, and, when built on moulds, the moulds next; the skin is then bent on to the inner keel, inwale, and moulds by the application of hot water, and made fast to the two former. This having been done, the boat in her then condition is turned over, right way uppermost, and firmly fixed on the stocks or frame; the timbers are thereupon put in, and the moulds removed as their places are thus supplied. Some builders, however, cut out the timbers by rule, and, using no moulds, fasten the skin at once on to them before turning the boat over. The stem and stern are made of solid pieces of wood—which is sometimes mahogany, cedar, or fir, at the option of the builder—and the skin worked up to them: the stem is usually strengthened and protected by a brass clamp; and the nails used are all made of copper. Besides the ordinary timbers, larger or "outrigged timbers" are inserted where the iron outriggers will be fixed, and to them the latter are fastened. They also aid in supporting one end of the thwart or frame on which the sliding seat works. The interior of the boat is divided into three portions by bulkheads, upon which are fastened the wooden decks, at whose upper corners are small holes for allowing the water to run out, when leaky, by turning the boat topsy-turvy. The breakwater rests upon the forward deck, and prevents rough and broken water from coming in. The coamings run round the sides of the boat to the coxswain's thwart, and crossing the boat abaft his seat, so end. The remainder of the boat is covered over with what is technically known as the canvas, but the covering is made of linen, well varnished, stretched, and nailed to the inwale. It is supported by a long strip of wood running longitudinally down the centre, and called the rising or ridge piece, and by crossbeams which run transversely from the rising piece to the inwale. The canvas is nailed on outside, through the skin to the inwale, and its edge is hidden by a thin beading which runs fore and aft.

The skin meets in the centre of the boat at the joints, and is fastened on to the inner keel; and there being no outer or visible keel, the bottom is round. The lengths of which the skin is composed are joined by "scarves," put in opposite one another. There are usually four scarves, two on each side; and the boat is thus divided into three lengths of skin, one long and two short, but this rule is not universal. The centre portion of racing boats is called the "body." All these boats are well varnished outside and in. The stretcher against which the rower's feet are placed is a strong piece of fir fitted into a rack with brass thumbscrews, and shifts according to length of leg; it should slope at a considerable angle towards the stern. Leather straps for the toes are fastened to it by small staples. In some boats there are bottom boards or burdens, and in others there are not. Temporary washboards made of strips of common deal wood 3in. or 4in. wide are occasionally fitted round the sides of racing boats, when the water is unusually rough, stretching out at right angles to the coamings and breakwater; and being merely tacked on can be removed as soon as the occasion for their use no longer exists.

The iron outriggers are made of four round stays; not many years since they were square, and the two lower or middle stays were then crossed. The two upper stays are the shortest, and, with the rowlock plate, are in one piece; the thowls, generally of beech wood cased with iron, are separate, and being fitted with shoulders through holes in the rowlock plate, receive the lower stays, fastened underneath by means of nuts. All four stays are fastened (at their lower extremities) through the outrigged timbers by means of nuts and bolts. There are likewise cross-stays inside the boat as occasion requires. Of the component parts of the rowlock, the forward thowl, or one rowed against, is called the "thowl," and the after one the "stopper," the oar resting on the bed or sill of the rowlock, which is generally made of hard wood. A piece of twisted string or wire crosses the top of the thowls to keep the oar or scull from jumping out of the rowlock, and is called the mousing—a nautical term for a piece of yarn used to turn round the mouth of a hook to prevent its unhooking: in America it sometimes takes the form of an iron rod, hinged on the top of the thowl, and fitting with a latch and a perpendicular spring to the top of the stopper, resting in a mortice, thus allowing an oarsman to raise the rod and unship his oar without passing the handle outboard.

In addition to the ordinary racing outrigger, there is a mongrel boat—a sort of compromise between the former and the old-fashioned craft—in request at the Universities and elsewhere. These boats are outrigged, but composed of several streaks of fir, with keels, and by reason of their greater weight, are chiefly used in preparing oarsmen for the lighter and faster kind; they are called tub-boats, and comprise eights, fours, and pairs. Inrigged gigs, in which the rowlock is on the gunwale, or walestreak, are also frequently made use of in instructing young hands, on account of their width and steadiness.

Twelve-oared cutters, of which there have been but four, are a comparative novelty, and have as yet only been built on the Tyne for the London Rowing Club, to aid in the selection and coaching of their Henley crew. The first one was constructed by Jewitt, of Dunston, to the order of Mr. H. H. Playford, about fifteen years ago. She was somewhat longer than an eight, but was curtailed more than she otherwise would have been, owing to the limited length of the club boathouse at Putney. The new twelve-oars now in use are 69ft. 8in. long, and 2ft. 3in. wide amidships, fitted with sliding seats.

Old-fashioned wager boats are only used by watermen and other professional rowers, as in the race for Doggett's Coat and Badge, and in occasional sculling matches, in which an express stipulation is made in the articles of agreement to that effect. Of late there has been so much latitude allowed in their construction, and several specimens recently turned out have approximated so closely to the modern sculling raceboat, with the exception of wooden batwings in lieu of iron outriggers, that endless objections and disputes have arisen on the occasions of their use. They should properly be built in not less than three streaks, with an outer keel. The lower or keel streak should not be *more* than 5in., and the other two streaks not *less* than $2\frac{1}{2}$in. each, in breadth at the thwart; the former may be made as much less than 5in., and the latter as much more than $2\frac{1}{2}$in. as the builder thinks fit. The boats should also have wooden saxboards and wooden chockheads; further than this no limitation can well be laid down. At the Thames National Regatta there was once a rule that in all *bonâ fide* old-fashioned wager boats constructed in not less than three streaks, a line or string drawn from the keel to the rowlock should touch each plank; but as the boats are now built, this is very far from being the case, for they resemble outriggers to a great extent, their sides being brought up sharply, and the timbers and wings which support the rowlocks flaring out at a considerable angle.

Non-coxswain fours have come into fashion in England during the last decade, although for some years previously they were in general use in America, from which country the invention was imported into the Old World, consequent upon the successful performance, in the Paris International Regatta of 1867, of the St. John's, New Brunswick, four-oared crew; whose victory was as much owing to their rowing without a coxswain as to the fact that, though ostensibly amateurs, they were in reality professional oarsmen competing on unduly favourable terms with amateur crews of England and the Continent, carrying coxswains. The first four-oared crew without a coxswain, and steered by a traveller on the stretcher of an oarsman, of which there is authentic record, rowed at the College Regatta at Springfield, Massachusetts, in 1855, between Harvard and Yale crews. Harvard started an eight-oar with a coxswain, and a four-oar without a coxswain, fitted with foot-steering gear. Yale started two six-oared crews, both with coxswains. The Harvard eight and four came in first and second, while the Yale sixes brought up the rear. The smaller boats were allowed a handicap of 11 seconds per oar for the three miles of the course; and after reckoning for the difference in time according to the handicap, the Harvard eight, with a steersman, only beat the College four, without a coxswain, by 3 seconds—44 seconds being deducted from the 47 seconds actual difference between the crews. The performance of the St. John's crew, at Paris, in 1867, forcibly impressed the

English rowing men who were present, with the enormous advantage a four-oar without a steersman possessed over a boat with one—the dead weight of the latter, amounting to several stone, being avoided, not to mention the unsteadiness of which a steersman is always the source in a four. Mr. W. B. Woodgate, of Brasenose College, Oxford, is entitled to the merit of taking the earliest advantage of the new system, for he had a non-coxswain four constructed for his college crew to row the race for the Stewards' Cup at Henley, in 1868, the year following the Paris Regatta. An objection having been lodged against this new boat competing on equal terms with crews steered in the usual manner, Mr. Woodgate had a temporary seat fitted on the after deck of his new fashioned four, and went to the post with his coxswain duly installed, to compete for the first trial heat against two crews from Surbiton. As soon as the signal was given, the Brasenose coxswain jumped overboard, and after considerable difficulty was rescued by some pleasure boats from the depths of Remenham Reach. Meanwhile Mr. Woodgate's four continued the race, and being well guided by the feet-steering gear came in first. It is almost unnecessary to add that the Brasenose crew were disqualified for not carrying a coxswain, according to the rules of the regatta, and the heat awarded to the boat which came in second. The incident, however, was not without its results later on.

We next find the Champion crew from the Tyne rowing against the St. John's crew at Lachine, in Canada, in 1870 (both using four oars without coxswains), and defeating them easily; and the London

Rowing Club, using a non-coxswain four with sliding seats, beat the New York Atalanta crew in a non-coxswain four with fixed seats, on the Thames, in June 1872, and shortly afterwards rowed over for a special prize for the new description of boat at the Henley Regatta the same year, the Atalanta crew withdrawing. Non-coxswain fours were first used at the Marlow Regatta in 1872, for the Stewards' Cup at Henley in 1873, and for the Visitors and Wyfold Cups in 1874, during which time they had come into general use in the United Kingdom.

Racing boats in America are for the most part made of paper or papier maché which not only does duty for, but closely resembles the cedar wood used in English boats, both in appearance and colour, and which in that country is believed to be more durable and stronger than wood, requiring as it does but few timbers in a boat built of it.

It is almost unnecessary to state that a boat rowed with oars has an equal number on both sides, so as to preserve a straight course. These oars number from the bow or front of the boat towards the stern or after part; thus, the first oar is called Bow, the second No. 2, and so on, Nos. 3, 4, 5, 6, 7, and the eighth, or last, Stroke, as it is rowed by the man who sets the time or stroke. The odd numbers constitute the right, starboard, or bow side, and the even numbers the left, port, or stroke side oars. This is the rule; the exception, which is very rare, is in the case of a few north-country boats, which carry the stroke on the right or starboard side, and the bow oars on the left, larboard, or port side. The terms starboard and port are, however, seldom or never applied to rowing-boats, but "bow side" or "stroke side," as the case may be. The coxswain, where there is one, sits on the aftermost thwart, or that nearest the stern of the boat, and faces the crew; he therefore looks towards the course he is travelling.

The oars and sculls should be made of the best white spruce fir, and consist of the handle, the loom, and the blade. The length of oars varies according to the description of boat in which they are used, say from 12ft. in pair-oars, to 12ft. 9in. in eight-oars; but wager-boat sculls should not be less than 10ft., or more than 10ft. 4in. long. Both are kept in their proper place in the rowlock by a circular button of a peculiar shape, on the leather, which plays against the inner side of the thowl. Under the old system the oars and sculls were square loomed; now they are round, and besides being much less noisy, are far easier to work with.

Rudders are fitted to eights and fours, and are made sometimes of cedar, mahogany, fir, and even oak. Across the top of the rudder, which is fastened to the sternpost with a pin and tubing, is a wooden or brass crosspiece or yoke, from each end of which a yoke or rudder-line passes (through rings on the top of the canvas and inwale) to the coxwain's thwart. This thwart should be made not less than a foot deep, so as to allow him to aid in trimming the boat by sitting on the forward or after part of it as occasion may require. On fours which do not carry coxwains, and occasionally on pair-oars and sculling boats, rudders are fitted in the usual way—varying, of course, in size, those of pairs and scullers' boats being very small. The yoke lines, instead of being made of cord, consist of twisted wire, and are carried along the gunwales, generally inside, but occasionally outside, the boat, one on each side to the stretcher of the oarsman—usually the bowman, or No. 2—who steers. They are fastened to a traveller, which the steerer works with his feet, pressing his right or left foot laterally to whichever side he wishes to direct the course of the boat, and so moving the yoke and the rudder accordingly.

The best mats for rowing upon are made of washleather stuffed with horsehair, or of plain sheepskin, but in boats fitted with sliding seats they are seldom or never used, the sliding seats being covered with green baize, or in some cases cork, whilst in others the oarsman sits on the bare wood.

The following table will show the average dimensions of modern single-streak racing boats. They do not differ very materially from the boats with fixed seats which preceded them, but in the latter the distance from thwart to thowl was 13 inches, which is still correct where no sliding seats are affixed. Tub-eights and fours, which are in frequent use for instructing beginners, are about 56ft. and 36ft. to 38ft. long respectively, the former with a breadth of from 2ft. 2in. to 2ft. 6in., and the latter with a beam of 2ft. 2in. to 2ft. 4in., but these are deeper and heavier than the racing craft. The distance from thwart to thowl is given on the next page as 5 inches, but it varies in different boats according to the fancy of the builders, and in some craft is much greater.

Dimensions of Modern Boats.

Particulars.	Racing Eight.		Racing Fours. With Cox.		Racing Fours. Without Cox.		Pair-oar.		Sculling Boat.	
	ft.	in.	ft.	in.	ft.	in.	ft.	in.	ft.	in.
Length of boat	58	6	41	0	40	0	34	4	30	0
Breadth (over all)	2	0	1	9	1	8	1	4⅝	1	4[illegible]†
Depth, amidships	1	1½	1	0½	1	0	0	10½	0	8½
Depth, stem...	0	8	0	7¼	0	7½	0	4¼	0	3½
Depth, stern	0	7¼	0	6¾	0	6½	0	3¾	0	2¾
Distance from seat to thowl*	0	5	0	5	0	5	0	4½	0	4
Height of work from level of slide...	0	7¾	0	7¾	0	7¾	0	7½	0	7½
Length of slide	1	4	1	4	1	4	1	5	1	5½
Length of amidship oars	12	6	12	6	12	6	...	...	...	...
Buttoned at...	3	6	3	5½	3	5½	...	...	...	...
Length of bow and stroke oars ...	12	4	12	4	12	4	12	3	...	...
Buttoned at...	3	4½	3	4½	3	4½	3	4	...	...
Length of sculls	...	...	...	...	...	...	...		10	0
Buttoned at...									2	8
Space between cox.'s thwart and stroke's stretcher (cox.'s thwart 18in. deep)	1	8	1	8	...	...	...		...	...

* Measured from front edge of slide to plane of thowl.

† Breadth on boat, 11¼in.

CHAPTER III.

The Sliding Seat: Its Invention, Adoption, and Theory.

The most important and most recent invention in regard to boat-rowing is unquestionably the sliding seat, which has improved the speed of the racing boat almost as much as the adoption of iron outriggers increased that of the old-fashioned in-rigged craft thirty or forty years ago; and it may be accounted for as follows. At the moment when the oar is striking the water to take the stroke, the muscles of the body and legs are animated with intense activity, and by their united exertions a portion of the weight of the body is brought into action as an element of propelling power. How much of this weight is actually called into play, and how much is left to be borne up by the thwart and the stretcher, depend entirely on the strength of these muscles, and the command over them which, by practice, the oarsman has acquired, to make them act promptly and with their maximum intensity, from the moment his oar enters the water until the blade is abaft the rowlock. If, as is the case with very few, and those the best oarsmen, these muscles in combination are capable of raising the whole weight of the body off the seat, then the maximum effect will be obtained; and though less experienced and physically weaker men may, for a brief period be able to accomplish this, it is rarely that such efforts can be long continued. Hence many, and especially inexperienced oarsmen fail to bring to their aid all the power due to their weight. It is evident that if means can be found to concentrate in the stroke the living force due to the whole muscular power of the individual, and to the utilization of the weight of the whole body moving over *the longest distance* which the structure of the boat and conformation of the oarsman will permit, a great gain has been acquired. Fortunately this has been discovered in the principle of the "sliding stroke," by means of the mechanism of the "sliding seat." While the theory of this stroke is correct, experience has proved that its use is attended with difficulties, which even constant practice cannot always overcome. The employment of this stroke led to the use of two kinds of seat, both designed to reduce to a minimum the friction due to the weight of the body. In the first of these the oarsman or sculler slid directly on a fixed seat, of a foot or more in length, well greased; but this plan has given way to one where the seat itself is movable, and upon which the operator sits, sliding backwards and forwards in a direction parallel to the kelson, upon an under or fixed thwart, by means of rails and runners—the seat moving with the oarsman, instead of the latter slipping to and fro upon an immovable thwart.

The originator of this sliding seat was an American oarsman, Mr. J. C. Babcock, of the Nassau Boat Club, of New York, who has stated* that the first sliding or movable seat of which there is any record was attached to a novel single scull craft which he built in Chicago in the year 1857, called the "Experiment;" but that he did not consider the idea he had matured of any practical use. About the year 1861 Walter Brown, the American sculler, used a sliding seat in a single scull boat, and for a time was sanguine of its success. Later on, however, he abandoned the slide, but in 1870 took to it again, and obtained letters patent, claiming it as his own invention. The slide was used for the first time by a crew rowing with oars in May, 1870, at the opening day of the Hudson Amateur Rowing Association at Pleasant Valley; and it came about in this wise. During the season of 1869 Mr. Babcock was called upon to organise a racing crew and put them aright in their boat. In determining the proper distance to place the rowlock abaft the fixed thwart, various authorities were consulted, and it was found, he says, to be anywhere from nine to fifteen inches—although distinctly stated in the first edition of this work, published in 1866, to be 13 inches. Experiments on these extremes proved that a nine inch stroke gave a splendidly easy catch, but a poor finish, and a fifteen inch stroke a poor catch, and all that could be desired for a finish. Both one could not have, so a happy medium of twelve inches was adopted. In the winter of 1869-70 he had a rowing apparatus constructed, with oars, stretchers, seats, &c., for use

---

* Authentic letters of 14th Dec. 1870, in the "American Oarsman's Manual," and 12th Dec. 1872, in the *New York Spirit of the Times.*

indoors, being a perfect counterpart of work in a boat. Further experiment was then made as to the most advantageous distance at which to fix the stroke, but with the inevitable result that to catch well and finish well, with the ordinary oar and leverage, the rowlock should be moved six inches back and forward each stroke. As this was impracticable, the idea of moving the seat occurred to him, and it was applied to the rowing apparatus with perfect success. In May, 1870, the sliding seats were fitted to a six-oared gig, and a crew of the Nassau Boat Club of New York made the first appearance on sliding seats of which there is any record. The seat used was a wooden frame about ten inches square, covered with leather, and grooved at the edges to slide on two brass tracks fastened on to a thwart of sufficient length to allow a slide of from ten inches to one foot, though it was then considered that the proper length of slide was from four to six inches. The ways required to be occasionally lubricated with lard, but still it was found that no stops or fastenings were necessary to keep the seat in position. After a season's fair trial the inventor became convinced that it required more skill to use the seat properly than the oar, thus making it doubly difficult to perfect a crew. The tendency of the beginner, he found, was to slide *too much* and *at the wrong time*, for the simple reason that to use the slide improperly was easy and pleasant, while to use it correctly was difficult and fatiguing; and it was fully as important that the crew should slide together as that they should row together, though the former was found to be less facile. Mr. Babcock says that taking into consideration the fact of the best oarsmen in the world, the Tyne crew, sliding when spurting, from four to six inches on a fixed seat, he came to the conclusion that the movable seat could only be considered a mechanical contrivance intended for a better accomplishment of the sliding movement in rowing; but he observes that the general impression among those persons who used it was that as it gave the legs an opportunity of being brought into more active use than before, it added an additional propelling power to the stroke. This impression as it subsequently turned out, was correct. The inventor says that the idea of developing any extra power by leg work never occurred to him, either as an object sought, or one that had been attained; and this, too, despite the fact that he found less difficulty in working his crew on the new seat than he anticipated, for they appeared to him to do better than on stationary seats, and seemed to apply more force in their work, though their form was far from perfect.

The curious part of the business is, that Mr. Babcock seemed to think that his invention was merely a minor auxiliary to the sliding stroke in rowing, as exhibited by the Tyne crew at Lachine, in 1870, who slid on their fixed seats; whereas the fact really is, that the movable seat is the key of the whole problem which the oarsmen of this country were unable to solve. Not only is it a mechanical gain, in that it enables a much longer stroke to be rowed through the water, with less difficulty, than on a fixed seat, but that it does away with the mechanical difficulty of friction; and it is a physical gain also, inasmuch as it enables more power to be applied than under the old system, through the medium of the sliding stroke, by means of the legs, which, owing to their cramped position in rowing on fixed seats, were debarred from exerting the whole force of which they are now known to be capable.

The theory of the sliding seat was explained in the fullest manner in the early spring of 1873 in the columns of the *Field* newspaper, by the editor, Mr. J. H. Walsh, F.R.C.S., who resolved, with the assistance of two amateurs, to test the plan thoroughly in the interests of "British Rural Sports" in general, and rowing in particular—first as to the alleged difficulty of learning to slide; next, as to the actual gain by its means. The place selected was the London Rowing Club Boathouse, at Putney, and the gentlemen who assisted him were Mr. F. S. Gulston and Mr. L. P. Brickwood, both of that club. The first of these two gentlemen was, perhaps, the most accomplished oarsman and best "slider" of the day, while the last, though an excellent sculler in former years, was quite innocent of practical knowledge of the sliding seat, which he had never used, having given up rowing for some time. The first experiment consisted in placing Mr. Brickwood afloat in Mr. Gulston's sculling boat, in which, although the stretcher was too short and the sculler quite out of practice, yet after a few minutes pulling he became perfectly at ease on the sliding seat, and a convert to its undoubted superiority over the old fashioned fixed seat; but there was nothing extraordinary in a rower who had been well taught on a fixed seat, becoming reconciled to the new invention almost immediately—*verbum sap.* The fact was established that the very act of using the straps to bring up the body after the conclusion of the stroke, draws the sliding seat forward, and that when this is followed by the pressure of the feet against the stretcher in rowing the stroke through the water, the rower is of necessity driven back to his former position. To the casual observer it would appear impossible to get the hands over and past the knees, which, when the body is fully forward, are drawn up considerably above the hands; but a close inspection will show that the arms, in reaching forward, pass the knees before the latter are raised to their full height, while in going backwards during the stroke the legs are straightened and the knees lowered before the hands approach them, the arms being unbent and at their fullest tension until after passing over the knees. A longer, and therefore a slower stroke than on a fixed seat resulted from the use of the new invention, with less effort than under the old plan, and at the same time with far less distress at the commencement of the recovery from a long swing back.

The next experiment consisted in having one of the new tub fours of the London Rowing Club laid on trestles and blocked up, so that an oarsman could sit on the thwart and pull an oar as he would if afloat. Mr. Gulston then took his seat at No. 2 thwart, and, having the assistance of two or three bystanders to hold the marks used, and to measure the distances, reached out as far as he could, giving himself some little impetus so as not to start from a dead point, to use a mechanical expression. He then went through the same movement with his oar in the air, as if it had been in the water. The spot where the stroke commenced was carefully marked with a rod, as well as the spot where it finished. The oar was then placed at right angles to the side of the boat, so as to be equi-distant from the thowl and stopper, and a mark was placed where the centre of the blade rested, thus giving the middle of the stroke. On measuring the distance between the commencement and the finish of the stroke, it was found that when using the sliding seat the total length of the stroke was 11ft. 7in. The distance from the commencement of the stroke to its centre opposite the rowlock was 6ft. 4½in., and from the centre to the finish 5ft. 2½in. This admeasurement was taken, not on the arc of the circle described by the blade of the oar, but on a straight line drawn from the commencement to the end of the stroke—the centre being found as above described, so that although it is not the line described by the blade of the oar, the proportion remains the same. The slide was then taken off the thwart of the tub-four, when Mr. Gulston, having considerably shortened his stretcher, and sitting further back than before, this time on the fixed thwart, rowed another stroke. The same process of measuring was repeated, when it was found that the stroke last rowed commenced almost at the identical spot as when rowed on the sliding seat, but the total length of stroke was only 10ft. 4in. against 11ft. 7in. The distance from the commencement to the centre was 6ft. 4in., making the forward part of the stroke half an inch less than that of the sliding seat, but the difference is so small that it practically amounts to the same thing. It was thus found that instead of the sliding seat giving, as was thought,

D

a longer forward reach than the fixed one, it gave practically the same; but in the afterpart of the stroke —that is, from the centre to the finish—the difference was most marked, for it gave 5ft. 2½in. against 4ft. on the fixed seat, the difference being 1ft. 2½ inches in favour of the last half of the stroke on a slide. Of course if the boat had been moving though the water, instead of as it was, a fixture on dry land, the length of stroke would have been greater in proportion to the speed of the boat.

The conclusion at which the editor of the *Field* arrived we cannot do better than give in his own words, for he is equally master of mechanics and anatomy:—" It has been found in rowing that a long, strong, and comparatively slow stroke of 34 or 36 will win over a distance, although it will be beaten in a spurt by a quick, sharp, and comparatively weak stroke of 42 or 44 to the minute. Hence length of stroke is to be desired—within certain limits. On the old seat a very long stroke could no doubt be given by the aid of great reach forward and corresponding swing; but of late years it has been found that this could easily be overdone—first, because the excessive swing causes the wooden boat, with its narrow floor, to dip too much for speed, next, because the power of the extensor muscles is applied disadvantageously both at the beginning and end of the very long stroke. By the measurement of Mr. Gulston's stroke on a sliding and on a fixed seat, it was found that the former was from 1ft. to 18in. the longer of the two, and that at the dip of his blade he could not only use his extensor muscles to advantage, but that he was enabled to finish at the

the oar has passed the knees, the wrists should be raised to bring the blade at right-angles to the water preparatory to dipping it, the fact of delaying this motion often resulting in not putting the oar in square. The body of the oarsman and the sliding seat are then drawn forward concurrently by the aid of the stretcher straps, in readiness for taking the stroke. Care must, however, be taken not to lower the hands too much, as this practice leads to chopping, and cutting the stroke. Men differ slightly in their length of reach, but everyone ought to be able to get the handle of his oar over his stretcher, and when there he should raise his hands straight up and at once, as if not raised at once the result is a hang, and if not straight the stroke is cut. The oar should then be instantaneously covered up to the shoulder, but no further; and immediately it is in this position the stroke should commence. The rower should "knit himself up," as the north country phrase is; he should then spring back like a bow when the string is loosed, and bring the muscles of his back and legs into play, as far as possible raising his weight off his seat—thus using his whole strength and weight at once and together. These motions at the end of the feather and the beginning of the stroke are, however, so simultaneous, and take place so rapidly, that it is very difficult to analyse them. It is in this part of the stroke that five minutes' looking at a good oarsman rowing, is worth more than any number of words; in fact, no words really convey what is wanted. A coach may tell his pupil to "hit" the water, to "smite" it,

&c., which may convey to the mind of a man who knows how to row what is required, but which can never impart the idea to a tyro. Catching the beginning properly—like swinging—must come from inspiration as it were. It will, however, assist a crew immensely if the coach will get into the boat, and row a few short spins at a slow stroke, employing all his power at the beginning, and making the crew follow his example; but he must be a strong man, as he will have the whole weight of the boat to lift at the commencement of the stroke.

Having thus learnt to catch the beginning of the stroke with his body only, the rower should finish it with his arms and shoulders, taking care to send his elbows close past his sides, and to drop his shoulders well down and back, keeping his head up, and his chest out. In the next place, the whole strength of his arms and shoulders should be put into the finish of the stroke. This may seem to be recommending the fault of rowing the stroke out at the end, but really it is not so. This fault arises either from the beginning of the stroke having been shirked, from not using the full force of the body, or from not bending the arms soon enough; if this happens, the body has to be kept waiting until the arms come up to it, and hence an unseemly jerk. It is very difficult to determine the exact period at which the arms are to be brought into play, but it ought to be done about the time that the body is perpendicular. Thus the full weight and strength of the rower will be applied, and the oar will be dashed through the water in the way that marks a good oarsman.

HOW TO USE AN OAR, AND SCULLS

The oar should be brought straight home to the chest, the root of the thumbs touching the body about an inch, or less, below the bottom of the breast-bone, where the ribs branch off; thus every inch of water is made use of. When there, the hands should be dropped straight down, and then be turned over and shot .out again close along the legs, and the body should follow without the least pause. If this be not done, the oar will be feathered under water, and the boat buried; water will be thrown on to the next oar, and the recovery impeded. In effecting the recovery the slide is an important agent, but before the forward sliding movement takes place, the body should be swung evenly forward from the hips—not with a jerk or a plunge, or quicker at one time than another, but freely and easily, as if the hip joint worked well, and not stiffly. Much benefit may be derived from watching two or three of the best oarsmen that can be found, observing them carefully—forming an ideal model, and then endeavouring to copy it.

Two or three points should particularly be borne in mind: First, that when the hands are raised at the commencement of the stroke, and the oar, *ipso facto*, struck down below the surface, the whole of the power should be brought to bear at the moment of the oar's contact with the water, so as to create the greatest effect in the first or vital part of the stroke—one of the most important and too frequently broken laws of rowing; secondly, that the pull home to the chest should be in a perfectly straight line, thus causing a horizontal stroke through the water, which is another law frequently disregarded; thirdly, that the finish of the stroke should be as quiet and easy as it is possible to make it, but without lessening the force applied, which naturally diminishes, because at the first part of the stroke, before the rowlock, the oar is at an acute angle to the boat, and after that at an obtuse angle. Here it is that one so often sees the stroke wind up with a jerk, as if to make some use of the little strength remaining in the human frame, the oar flirted out of the water, the elbows dug sharply back in an awkward and ungainly manner, and the body harshly and suddenly jolted forward.

Next in importance are the movements described by the oar itself, starting from a state of rest, *i.e.*, feathered, and at right-angles to the keel of the boat.

When the forward reach is taken, the blade of the oar should travel backwards in the air, horizontally, at the distance of a few inches from the surface of the water—of course depending upon the state of the surface, whether smooth or rough—until dipped for the stroke. As regards this dip, it is imperative that the blade descend to the proper depth before any force is applied, otherwise the stroke will be cut. To effect this, the hands must be raised sharply, and the stroke must be instantaneously commenced. In a word, the oar must be put into the water with energy—not suffered to drop in of its own weight. When on the feather, the oar, after passing the knees, should be gradually turned preparatory to immersion, the feather concluding and the stroke beginning at once, with no interval whatever. Hence it will be perceived that the line described by the end of the blade, about which there are numerous theories and a variety of opinions,

HOW TO USE AN OAR, AND SCULLS. 51

will be nearly parallel with the water until entering it, when it will immediately be dipped with a *powerful scoop*.

The entry of the oar into the water cannot be too sudden or too decided, so that it be not a chop and a splash; and for this purpose the muscles of the arms should be gathering themselves together as the hands reach forward. It is a well-known and indisputable law that the greatest power can be applied in the first half of the stroke, that is to say, before the oar comes level with or abreast of the rowlock, and that the further aft it goes subsequently to passing that point, the more that power decreases. Such being the case, it is only an act of common sense to endeavour to do as much work as possible when it will tell most, and when it contributes to lift a boat lightly along the top of the water. On the other hand, if the application of the strength is deferred until the last part of the stroke, it is brought to bear when it is of least service; a great and useless expenditure of power ensues, and the boat, instead of being assisted over the water, is driven down and buried in it, her way being thereby checked. The same result ensues from men letting their weight rest on the seat, and then giving a wrench and feathering under water, instead of letting the weight rest on the stretcher and handle of the oar —in a word, from rowing with the arms rather than with the body, instead of using both.

We now come to the position in which the blade is immersed, and I would observe that this is a most important point. It is said that the blade should descend at right-angles to the water. In this opinion

I cannot altogether coincide, although even such a position is far superior to an entry with the back of the blade forming an acute angle with the water, and the front of the blade an obtuse one. In either of these cases, however, there is something wrong with the thowl rowed against, with the side of the loom which bears against the thowl, or with that on which the oar rests when traversing the water. The proper position is for the front or hollow of the blade to be looking slightly downwards upon, not along, the surface; its entry is consequently at less than a right-angle. This enables the oar to take full and square hold of the water at once; it prevents it running down too deep, and, if firmly and scientifically manipulated, it obviates splashing. At the same time the oar ought not to be turned over too much, as otherwise it will not enter the water easily, and will be apt to twist in the hand, besides straining the wrists; but no effort whatever should be made to force it over. The depth to which the oar descends through the medium of this peculiar catch, is to the shoulder or upper end of the blade. In this position it must continue until the hands are up to the chest — not stopping at the distance of a foot from it—when the stroke is concluded, and the feather commences. In its traverse through the water the blade of an oar should be barely covered, and no more—this is an accepted rule — and, with the extraordinarily light boats used at the present day, strict attention to this principle must be paid. When bringing the stroke to an end, the blade of the oar, by a sudden movement — caused by dropping the hands and turning the wrists—is feathered or brought into a plane with the surface of the water, from being previously at right-angles to it. This action should take place at the moment when the oar leaves the water, and the lower end of the blade, by being suddenly turned cleanly aft as the loom rotates in the rowlock, throws the water astern in a little eddying whirlpool, and the whole business of the stroke is completed. The appearance of this whirlpool should be carefully studied, as it is a pretty good criterion how a man is rowing; and if a coach happens to be pulling himself, as is occasionally the case, it is one of the only guides he has in judging how his pupils are rowing behind him. It is almost impossible to describe the look it ought to wear, but plenty of small air-bubbles should keep rising, as in a soda-water bottle, long after the swirl has left the oar: the smaller eddies should be deep and well marked. Very light rowing makes a splash that soon subsides, and deep rowing shows no air-bubbles.

The foregoing component parts of a stroke and its succeeding feather, it must be admitted, are numerous, and to a certain extent apparently incompatible; but yet they are so blended in the work done by an expert oarsman as to seem but one action. Each, however, is fully and correctly performed, and the sum of these separate actions is consequently also perfect.

At the risk of appearing prolix, I will briefly recapitulate the main points to be recollected. They are as follows : First, a full, fair reach-out over the toes, with both arms perfectly straight ; secondly, a square hold of the water at the dip of the oar, with an application of the whole power at the moment of immersion; thirdly, a firm stroke of a medium depth, pulled straight through the water without wavering and without vibration, yet always kept long and duly light; fourthly, a graceful, easy finish, with a clean turn of the water off the after-edge of the blade—the feather being light, moderately low, and rapid—and an instantaneous movement when the oar completes the feather, and descends under water.

Besides pulling, which, as before stated, does not constitute the whole science of rowing, there are various manœuvres of which a knowledge is necessary; these are *paddling, easing, holding water*, and *backing*.

Paddling is simply a milder form of rowing hard, of which the opposite extreme is spurting. The difference consists merely in the strength applied, and consequently in the number of strokes taken to the minute: it is, without question, the form most suitable for discovering and correcting faults, and it is, therefore, peculiarly valuable for the purpose of coaching crews which have races to row, especially over long distances.

Easing signifies either a reduction in speed from rowing hard to paddling, or else ceasing to row altogether. More commonly, however, it denotes a cessation of rowing, the command "Easy all" being generally understood to mean "Leave off pulling." Should it be desired merely to reduce the speed, the usual term employed is "Row easy all." Herein consists the difference between this order and that of "Easy all," which should always be given before the conclusion, or, more correctly speaking, immediately after the commencement of a stroke.

HOW TO USE AN OAR, AND SCULLS. 55

Holding water is the act of stopping a boat suddenly, and is accomplished by partially reversing the oar and running it down under the water, so as to check her way; but the oar should be held, when deeply immersed, with the blade nearly in the same position as on the feather, but under instead of above the water—certainly not at right-angles to it. By a simple twist of the handle from or to the body, the blade can be raised or lowered according as it is found necessary to slacken or increase the power exerted to check the boat; that is to say, by simply turning the blade with its upper edge downwards towards the nose of the boat, the oar sinks, and by depressing the after or lower edge, it immediately rises to the surface of the water.

Backing is exactly the opposite of rowing, and is accomplished by reversing the oar, as in the last-mentioned manœuvre, and pushing instead of pulling the handle. The same principles which apply to rowing apply here also, for the blade should never be sunk too deep, but the back stroke through the water should be long and light, and the oar should be feathered, and carried on the feather, exactly as when pulling in the ordinary manner, although in a contrary direction. The action is commenced with the body well back, and is finished but little beyond the knees; here, again, the first being the vital part of the stroke.

Rowing and backing a boat round should, however, be done as gently as possible, for nothing screws an outrigger so much as the application of force under these circumstances. If this is attended to, a boat will last twice as long as she otherwise would.

The celerity with which these various movements can

be performed, must be acquired by practice, and a rapid change from one to the other can only be skilfully executed after much experience. Theory is all very well as a guide, but actual practice and manipulation are the only things capable of rendering a man thoroughly conversant with these technicalities.

When about to disembark, the oar should be unshipped, and lifted out before leaving the boat.

How to Scull.

Sculling, as already mentioned, is usually performed by one person, who sits in the centre of the thwart and boat, and uses a pair of short oars technically called "sculls," one in each hand. Double sculling has recently come more or less into fashion, and is performed by two persons instead of one; the boat used being similar to a pair-oared wager boat, but with two pairs of outriggers for a corresponding number of sculls, instead of one pair for oars.

In holding the sculls it is a mere matter of fancy whether the right hand or the left hand is uppermost, the sculls overlapping more or less. Some men prefer one hand and some the other, but whichever plan seems easiest and most natural should be followed. The great points to be borne in mind are, to sit upright, to reach out well over the toes, dropping the body between the knees, which should open out as the arms stretch forward; to get firm hold of the water at the moment of contact—as explained in connection with the oar—and to lift the boat *over* the water with the first part of the stroke. The power applied will of itself gradually diminish as the stroke is brought to an end; but the "seaman's dig" and jerk should above all things be avoided, as no boat is so susceptible of downward pressure as a thin, frail, sculling outrigger. The elbows should be kept close to the flanks; the body should not fall back too far; the blades of the sculls should clear the water when on the feather; and the pick-up of the body in the recovery should be rapid. In a word, the main principles to be attended to are the same as in rowing an oar. A sculling-boat may be stopped almost dead—in less time than it takes to relate it—by running the sculls down under water in the same manner as the oar; and backing water is precisely similar, only with two sculls instead of one oar. To turn, one scull is backed and the other pulled. The sculls when not in use should invariably lie flat on the water, to preserve the equilibrium of the boat.

The great art is to pull equally and evenly with both hands in order to balance the boat and maintain a straight course, for, there being no coxswain, the sculler has to do his own steering. This he accomplishes partly by keeping the stern of his boat pointed straight to some fixed object astern, and partly by turning his head—not his shoulders or body—round to the right or left, to enable him to cast his right or left eye, as the case may be, as far along the water in front as possible. At best it is a difficult matter to keep a straight course, and to do it well can only be acquired by long practice. In a race, where men are always more or less under the influence of excitement, the difficulty of steering is even more apparent, and it frequently contributes to defeat, as incompetence in this respect, on the part of a competitor, can never be altogether counterbalanced by the verbal directions of a pilot afloat or ashore. As to the rate of stroke, he is no mean sculler who can pull thirty-five or thirty-six thorough strokes in a minute. And in rough water, this rate will be somewhat lessened, for the longer the stroke and the higher the feather, so as to clear the surf, the better.

CHAPTER V.

FAULTS AND ERRORS: WHAT TO AVOID.

THERE are two kinds of faults connected with the art of rowing, and they are as follows: First, errors of position and appearance, which, although ungainly and slovenly in themselves, do not prejudicially affect the progress made; and, secondly, faults of labour, or errors connected with an improper use of the oar and sliding seat, which militate against the speed of the boat, as well as against an efficient performance of work. By far the greater part of them come from men not holding their oars properly, and not having good seats; yet how very seldom are they taught either one or the other.

The chief errors of position and form consist of sitting askew, with rounded shoulders, head down, body sunk in and dropped, knees close together, with the outside hand capping the oar, and the inner hand too far off the outer; of shoulders out of a level; reaching out without letting the body come well between the legs; over-reaching; looking out of the boat, and at the oar; staring about (perfectly inexcusable in an eight); dropping the head; throwing the head backwards and forwards when at work, as if it hung on an easy and well-used hinge; meeting the oar—attributable to not swinging far enough, not keeping the chest and stomach out, and not using the muscles of the latter; feathering too high or too low; failing to row fore and aft, but rolling across the boat, generally away from the oar—called rowing out of the boat—and screwing; beginning at one side, rowing round, and finishing with the body on the same side; sticking the elbows out at the end of the stroke, and falling back too far, or not sufficiently, beyond the perpendicular. There is also a bad habit of letting the oar remain in an improper position when feathered, if the boat is lying still, or driving with her own way, such as keeping the blade off the water and in the air, with the handle low down in the boat.

Next come faults of labour, and they are numerous; many of them, also, are beyond measure subtle. First and foremost is that of not straightening the arms when reaching out. In this case both wrists are generally in the same position, that is to say, either convex or flat, instead of one in each. One arm—the inner—is also usually crooked, and one—the outer—straight. Consequently, when the oar catches the water, the whole of the weight is thrown upon one arm, or else the stroke is not begun at the proper time or with full purchase, and the water is laid hold of comparatively late, and so the opportunity of getting the earliest and lightest lift on the boat is neglected. Secondly, that of sliding too soon, before the full weight of the body is applied to the oar, or the swinging back well commenced—the result being loss of power;

FAULTS AND ERRORS.   61

and there is, unquestionably, a great tendency to this error on the part of men who have not been well taught to row on a fixed seat. Thirdly, those of not holding the oar tight; of dropping the hands very low when reaching out, and so raising the blade too high on the feather; pausing or dwelling in the air before beginning a stroke, generally consequent upon the previously mentioned error of dropping the hands too much; dipping the blade quietly and indecisively, or letting it fall into the water, and pulling after it has attained a certain depth in its downward course, and when nearly level with the rowlock, or abeam; rowing the stroke through with a vibratory motion, or, as it were, making two distinct or separate pulls, instead of one firm, clean, decided stroke—commonly a sign of weakness, or of too much muscle in the arms, men accustomed to gymnastics usually doing it; bringing the hands high up, over, and down again, like turning a mangle, the hand rising as the blade descends, and being subsequently pulled violently downwards so as forcibly to clear the blade from the water, instead of a long, easy, light sweep—and finishing the stroke with the oar a long distance off the chest, instead of touching it. Beside these are jerking, compassed either by an uneven and jerky entrance of the oar into the water, or fetching the body up suddenly before concluding the stroke; doubling up over the oar, and at the same time flirting the oar out of the water with a sudden jolt of the arms; dipping the oar into the water, with its face forming an obtuse angle with the surface, when it often runs down deep under water, and the momentum of the boat and the resistance of the water driving the blade astern, overpower the oarsman, and nine times out of ten knock him backwards off his thwart—called catching a crab. Catching crabs also frequently results from not clearing the blade at the end of a stroke, or from not carrying it back at a sufficient height above the water, when, without sufficient warning, and in an instant, a wave comes, and the oar is whirled out of the control and, maybe, hands of its wielder, and sometimes breaks, the rowlock more frequently giving way. It is seldom, however, that men catch regular crabs in an eight, but they very frequently cut through the water in coming forward— a fault that arises from not dropping the hands sufficiently on the feather. It is by no means a trivial fault, as it throws water on to the blade of the next man on the same side, and occasionally leads to a broken oar.

Of all faults, perhaps the most common, and one of the most difficult to discern, is that of shirking. Now, shirking may take place either at the beginning or end of the stroke, or both. At the beginning of the stroke it is more likely to pass muster, and is, therefore, more frequently adopted, especially by men who can really row well, but who, for the time being, either through laziness or because they are not quite up to the mark, are desirous of sparing themselves; and so cunningly may this be done by a clever oarsman, that ninety-nine out of every hundred persons who witnessed the performance would not discover anything amiss, especially as the sliding seat easily aids in the deception. A less experienced man than the offender would scarcely be capable of detecting the error, and

FAULTS AND ERRORS. 63

of fixing it upon the guilty party. It consists in abstaining from bringing the whole of the power to bear at the moment of the oar's contact with the water, by rowing with unstraightened arms, or, rather, slackened muscles—thus quite putting aside that firm grip of the water which is so essential a qualification of correct work—when, although the oar may be dipped simultaneously with others, and apparently with as much effect, the strength is not actually laid out until the weight of the boat is already lifted by those men who are doing their work as honestly as willingly; and even then only partially so. At the end of the stroke the shirker finishes his work before anyone else in the boat, being the first to commence the feather, as well as the last to begin the actual labour; his oar may enter and leave the water at the same time as the rest, but though keeping time he is not following the stroke, the work of those who do keep stroke being uniform and simultaneous. The best way to detect this fault is to look at the water that comes from the suspected oar; it cannot present the proper appearance if the rower is shirking. At the same time, the converse does not hold good, for a man may be rowing too deep. Rowing very light is shirking.

Among other tricks that should be avoided, I may mention those of throwing up on to succeeding oars the water which should be turned aft off the lower end of the blade, as the oar is feathered—for, if thrown up, the wash falls upon the back of the next oar on the same side, and grievously incommodes the man who is rowing it, even if it does not actually knock it out of his hand; feathering too soon and under water, which is a most productive source of crab-catching; feathering and returning, that is to say, simply feathering and then carrying the oar back unfeathered, or bringing the blade momentarily into a plane with the surface of the water, and then as suddenly turning it back again until at right angles thereto—thus not only spoiling the appearance of a boat, but positively doing it an injury by offering an unnecessary resistance to the wind, besides incurring the risk of catching the water; letting the oar fall on the water, after feathering, with a pat, and so not only hindering the boat's way, but provoking crabs. In many cases this habit is prolonged into a continued dribbling of the oar along the surface of the water, when feathered—frequently witnessed in pair-oared rowing, and usually the sign of a want of balance in the boat. Occasionally, too, the hands are not sufficiently lowered as the feather is being brought to an end before taking a stroke, and the inferior corner of the oar knocks up water and splashes in consequence. Neither is the entry of the oar into the water always firm or decided enough; nor should its face be turned up, but on the contrary, downwards, as previously explained.

Finally, the body is not always swung sufficiently well fore and aft, nor are the muscles of the hips and legs brought into play upon the seat and against the stretcher as they should be, but advantage is taken of the sliding movement to evade the crucial grip of the water at the exact period when it is invaluable. Now the lift and power applied to the first part of the stroke ought not to be prejudicially affected in the slightest degree by the movable seat, the use of which does not prevent an oarsman from applying as much skill and strength to the beginning of the stroke as on a fixed seat, for the sliding seat only commences to move backwards as the body reaches the perpendicular, by which time the stroke ought to be not only well begun, but half done.

Bad watermanship or want of watermanship is a very common fault, but it is more frequent among University oarsmen than among those of the London Clubs. Nothing leads to good watermanship so much as continual practice in a sculling boat, by which a man soon becomes competent to guide and manage a boat in difficulties as well as out of them; and this is probably the reason why rowing men on the lower portions of the Thames are so much more handy in a boat than those at the Universities and public schools, where eight-oared rowing is the rule, and sculling the exception. The knack of sitting a boat and of helping to steady it when rolling in a surf, or of counterbalancing a lurch caused by another oarsman in the crew, is a most valuable acquisition, but is possessed by very few. To acquire it, long practice, amounting to a complete apprenticeship, if it may be so termed, is necessary, as well as to enable a man to discover when anything is out of order, and to rectify it.

CHAPTER VI.

STEERING: COXSWAIN AND NON-COXSWAIN.

WHETHER a boat be guided by a coxswain or by an oarsman in the crew, the task of steering is by no means the least important one to be performed in a race, since much depends on a boat's course being the shortest practicable; and many opportunities occur where a coolheaded and clever steersman may gain a marked advantage, and perhaps attain absolute success. The general duties of the steersman, whether he be a coxswain, or an oarsman using a mechanical steering apparatus, are in themselves simple; hence it is commonly supposed that anyone can fill the place, particularly that of a coxswain, and perform properly all the minutiæ of the office. Yet, simple as they are, there is an ample field for the exercise of talent on the part of the operator. These duties are to control the movements and actions of a crew, by giving the requisite orders for starting, easing, or stopping, and especially to keep the boat in the straightest or best course, without any unnecessary deviations or wasteful exercise of the powers of the oarsman. Unfortunately, however, they are often most inefficiently performed.

STEERING.

At the present day the coxswain does little else but guide the boat, because it is the prevailing fashion to have a coach with each crew until they row their race; and this person exercises many of the functions which were formerly the part of the handler of the yoke-lines. Coxswains are consequently chosen for their light weight and small stature; but, excepting in very special cases, this "feather" weight is too often accompanied by want of judgment—not to say knowledge—and especially by want of decision and presence of mind in moments of danger and difficulty. At the same time, if a coxswain can be found combining in his own proper person, lightness of weight, a minute knowledge of rowing, a clear and cool head, with an unerring eye, he is a most valuable acquisition—he is the beau ideal of a coxswain. On the other hand, it is far better to carry a stone or two of extra weight, combined with these qualities, than to put at the yoke-lines a mere child without discretion or discrimination. Not seldom do we see races hanging in the balance, utterly thrown away by a sudden sheer to the right or the left, when the exercise of a fragment of judgment, and an appeal to the crew for a spurt at the nick of time, would land them winners by a yard.

The coxswain should take up his position on the aftermost thwart, upon which he should sit upright, with his body tilted slightly forward, his legs crossed, tailor fashion, and brought as close under him as possible, each foot resting sideways on its outer edge, and his knees wide apart. The yoke-lines should be stretched quite taut, and be held one in each hand, with a single turn round the palm; and there is usually a loop tied in each line, for the insertion of the thumb. Sometimes the thumbs are put in the loops without taking a turn of the line round the hand, but in every case the lines should be fastened together in front of the coxswain's body—even if they are not made of one piece, which seldom happens—or to the sides of the boat, otherwise by a sudden lurch, or from some other accidental cause, one of them may go overboard and tow astern—a *contretemps* by all means to be avoided. The coxswain's hands may rest one on each gunwale, the thumbs being inside, and the fingers outside. This enables him to balance himself, and to assist in steadying the boat; and, by a simple turn of the wrist, he can tighten or slacken the line he wishes. A coxswain can thus steer just as well, and can keep quite as true a course, as by holding the lines in any other manner, always providing he keeps them taut, which is essential. Another way of holding the strings is with the hands in the lap; but in either case the knees, by resting on the gunwales, contribute to regulate the body of the coxswain, which too often renders the after part of the boat top-heavy and unsteady. The coxswain should ease himself forwards, with the slightest possible departure from an upright position, at every stroke. The lift of the boat will guide him correctly enough; but he must especially be careful never to bob backwards and forwards, after the absurd and erroneous fashion of days gone by.

The words of command that are commonly used in directing a crew are few, and the fewer the better. The

STEERING. 69

same terms should always be employed, as there is then no chance of being misunderstood; but various localities have various practices. When starting a crew in an ordinary sort of way—although it is frequently necessary for bow and No. 3, or 2 and 4, to pull a stroke—the coxswain generally says, "Are you all ready?" followed by "Row on, all!" but on the London water these instructions are divided into three—*i.e.*, "Are you ready?" "Get forward, all," and then "Go!" This may be all very well in a race or in practising starts; but it is preferable to economise words. When it is necessary to diminish the pace, but not to cease rowing, the term "Row easy, all" is employed, or "Row easy, bow side," or "stroke side," as the case may be; but when discontinuing pulling, "Easy, all," at which command everyone ceases to row. This last order should be given at an appreciable interval before the conclusion of a stroke, so as to prevent the crew from commencing another. When deemed desirable to stop the boat suddenly, the coxswain should say "Hold water," or "Hold her up, all," or "Stop her up, all;" and this may be followed, when her way is checked, by "Back water, all;" in turning round, "Pull, bow side, back, stroke side," or *vice versâ*, or "Bow and 3 row," and so on, according to requirements; "Easy all," or "Easy, bow and 3," as the case may be, bringing them again into a state of rest. In the event of getting too close to an obstruction, such as another boat, a barge, bridge, or the bank, so that there is a chance of the oars on one side touching it, the attention of the men wielding those particular oars may be called to the fact by the words, "Oars, bow side," or "stroke side;" or

"Mind your oars, bow side," &c. The former is the shortest, and therefore the best.

In steering a boat when the course is straight, the coxswain should take for his mark to be steered to, the most conspicuous object in the proper direction in which he is to go; but the further it is off the better. A chimney, a craft at anchor, a tree, a house, or any other equally visible mark, will serve his purpose. When, however, the stream takes a turn in the distance, the boat's head should be guided straight to the supposed point in the water at which she will commence to make her bend, but yet wide of the corner; and any notable but distant object in this line will be the correct mark to aim at until close to the promontory. The boat's head should not be brought round until nearly opposite the apex of the bend; but the main point to be recollected is to fetch a boat round gradually and by slow degrees, because the greater the application of the rudder, the greater the diminution of speed: in some cases it is even advisable to ease the oars on the inner side of the boat, or to call upon the outer side for an increased effort. The following maxim, however, is well worth remembering, viz., that "a boat should be 'coaxed' by its rudder;" and by judiciously increasing the pressure on the tightened line when the oars are out of the water, and slackening it when they are being pulled through the water, the labour of the men is lightened. It is only permissible to jam a rudder hard up, or hard down, when turning a sharp corner, as at the Universities, or in cases of threatened collision, or to wash a boat off.

The reason for coming up wide to a corner is sufficiently obvious, viz., to pass clear of the point without the necessity of pulling first one line and then the other; for, if a boat's nose were steered straight to a corner, the rudder would have to be used just before reaching it, to sheer her head out sufficiently to clear it, and immediately afterwards it would again have to be put on the opposite way, so as to follow the true course. A zigzag, instead of a regular, steady bend, would be the result, and ground would be thereby lost. To obviate this, a boat's head should always point towards the shore opposite to the corner round which she is travelling—and correctly so, for the reason I have just indicated, notwithstanding, at first sight, it may appear somewhat strange.

The most difficult time for steering is during a strong cross-wind, because a boat drives away rapidly to leeward. Under these circumstances, it will be necessary to keep her head slightly to windward of her true course—experience in the force of the wind will alone determine how much; consequently, her line of keel will not be coincident with the line of motion. Should the wind happen to be abeam, or on the quarter, the stern of the boat will be driven to leeward, and her head be brought up to windward; this must be counterbalanced by a proportionate use of the lee-line, always bearing in mind that the stern is more powerfully acted upon by the wind than the bow.

When a crew is being prepared for a particular race it is as well to let the coxswain have almost as much practice as the oarsmen; they will then get accustomed to one another, and if of an inquiring turn of mind, and of quick apprehension, he will soon learn to pick out any little fault that may pass unnoticed from the bank, and thereby will exercise a double check over his men. He will naturally make the most of every opportunity to study the set of the tide or current, and will use his best endeavours to pick up items of information from persons qualified to advise him on the point. The ordinary rule is to keep close to the banks when against the stream, and nearly in the centre when with it; but particular courses require special directions, into which it is not my purpose to enter, if I make two exceptions—these are the Putney and Henley courses. In regard to the course to be steered between Putney and Mortlake, the best plan is to make for Craven Cottage Point, rounding it rather closely, but avoiding getting in under the Fulham bank between Putney Bridge and that landmark; thence in nearly a straight line to the Soapworks Point, which should not be passed too wide; through the Surrey arch of Hammersmith Bridge, and close in until opposite the bottom of Chiswick Eyot, off which the best position is at a third of the width of the river from the towpath, giving the corner opposite Chiswick Church a moderately wide berth: thence in midstream until off the Bathing Creek on the righthand side, and then at the distance of a third of the width of the stream from the Middlesex bank to the Ship, taking the shore arch of Barnes Bridge, and keeping close to the buttress. Concerning the proper arch of Hammersmith Bridge to pass through, it may be observed that if the course of a boat is kept all along for the centre span—coming wide round the Soapworks corner—it does not signify much if that arch is taken, but the boat must not be pointed first for the Surrey arch, and then be suddenly changed for the centre, as has occasionally been done. Nevertheless, distance is undoubtedly saved by taking the shore arch, especially if on a good threequarters flood. It is simply necessary to go afloat and watch the set of the tide when running up, and to note the awkward position in which the steamboat pier and buttress are situated for a boat intending to take the centre arch, to be convinced of the justice of these remarks. Unless brought unusually wide round the bend off the Soapfactory, a boat must be thrown athwart the tide to pass on the Middlesex side of the pier. Down with the ebb the course should be kept nearly in midstream until passing the bottom of Chiswick Eyot, where the boat should be steered slightly to the Middlesex side of the centre until off the Doves; thence in midstream to Hammersmith Bridge, which should be passed pretty close to the Surrey buttress or steamboat-pier; and about midstream to Putney Bridge, unless the tide is very low, when the towpath shore should be hugged from the Crab Tree until arriving at Craven Cottage; thence in midstream to the Aqueduct. A voyage in one of the steamers which ply for hire in the summer-time is an easy way of finding the channel, for they always follow it, unless the river is very full.

At Henley the course to be kept is in midstream (or according to position at starting) until nearing Poplar Point, when the towpath bank should be hugged quite close until halfway up the last straight reach, when the second arch of the bridge from the Berkshire side should be aimed at. The towpath side is generally considered the best at starting—that is to say, in the absence of wind, or if there is a breeze off the Berkshire shore; but the centre of the river is the preferable course, unless a gale blows down the reach or off the Buckinghamshire bank, when the shelter of the bushes on that side may be sought and cultivated for three-quarters of a mile.

Where a foot steering apparatus is used, and the boat guided by one of the oarsmen in a crew, the man who steers should not fail before embarking to see that the wires connecting the rudder-yoke and traveller, or foot-steering gear, are all in order; so that the rudder, when not in action, may be in a direct line with the keel, offering the least possible resistance to the progress of the boat. In keeping the boat straight, some fixed object directly astern must be chosen, and the boat's after end kept directly in a line with it. The head of the steersman must be turned to one side or the other, as may seem easiest, for the purpose of keeping clear of obstructions, as mentioned in the observations on sculling in a preceding chapter; and by pressing the side of his foot laterally upon the right or left horn of the traveller, he tightens the yoke line to be acted upon, the rudder is forced over, and the boat's head guided in the required direction. A removal of the pressure of the foot releases the rudder, which returns to its normal position.

It is almost unnecessary to mention that no steersman should allow himself to be bored out of his course by an adversary, but it is much better to give way than to assist in bringing about a foul. This, however, must not be understood to mean that one is always to yield to such conduct, for if, on being cautioned, the opposing steersman persists in boring, and causes a foul, he does so at his own peril, and must take the consequences. In a difficulty, the steersman has to depend upon his own judgment; but his mind should promptly be made up, and his determination as promptly be acted upon. Perhaps one of the most awkward things to allow for, and pass, is a sailing barge making short boards across the course of a racing boat, and an inexperienced and nervous coxswain is apt to make a mess of it. The intervening distance between the two craft, and their respective rates of progression, should be calculated to a nicety in deciding upon the proper course to be taken.

Lastly, a knowledge of the mysteries of giving an antagonist the wash, by getting a rapid lead, is only to be gained by repeated practice; but the large wave travelling at a tangent from a boat's quarter, if judiciously thrown upon the bow or side of the enemy, will grievously prejudice their chance, even if in other respects the crews are pretty well matched.

The *rule of the road,* though the last is not the least important point on which a few plain instructions to steersmen are needed, with the view of diminishing the chances of collision on the water, and obviating the uncertainty which prevails in too many quarters. The following directions are founded on the practice which has become the custom of the day; where reasonable doubts exist, the rule of the road at sea is followed.

It has been previously been explained that "larboard" or "port" means lefthand, and "starboard" right hand, and the effect of putting a vessel's helm to the left, or "porting the helm," as it is called, is to make her turn to the right. The invariable rule in the case of ships at sea meeting end-on is that they are to pass on the larboard or port side of each other, each vessel keeping to the right. This result is attained by putting the helm to port, by which the rudder is starboarded, and the vessel's head turned to the right. The rule in the case of one vessel overtaking another is that the former shall keep out of the way of the latter. In row-boats it is assumed that the yoke-lines are never crossed, or if so that they are *double*-crossed (as round a pulley on the canvas of a racing-craft), and consequently in order to comply with the invariable rule of "porting the helm," a row boat steered with yoke-lines must pull the right or starboard line (looking towards the bow), but one steered with a tiller must "port its helm," or push it to the left hand. In both cases the course of the boat is the same, viz., to starboard or to the right, and the rule of the sea is thereby complied with.

1. A row-boat going against the stream or tide should take the shore or bank—which bank is immaterial—and should keep inside all boats meeting it.

2. A row-boat going with stream or tide should take a course in mid-river, and should keep outside all boats meeting it.

STEERING.

3. A row-boat overtaking another boat proceeding in the same direction should keep clear of the boat it overtakes, which should maintain its course.

4. A row-boat meeting another end-on in still or open waters or lakes, should keep to the right, as in walking, leaving the boat passed on the port or left side.

5. A row-boat with a coxswain should give way to a boat without a coxswain, subject to the foregoing rules in so far as they apply.

6. A boat towing with stream or tide should give way to a boat towing against it, and if it becomes necessary to unship or drop a tow line, the former should give way to the latter; but when a barge towing is passed by a pleasure boat towing, the latter should give way and go outside, as a small boat is the easier of the two to manage, in addition to which the river is the barge's highway.

7. A row-boat must give way to a sailing boat.

8. When a row-boat and a steamer pass each other, their actions should, as a rule, be governed by the same principle as on two row-boats passing; but in shallow waters the greater draught of the steam vessel should be remembered, and the row-boat give way to her.

It is the usual practice on the river for a pair-oar to give way to a four-oar, and a four-oar to an eight-oar, more perhaps as a matter of courtesy than from any strict right.

CHAPTER VII.

Teaching Beginners.

Some men are more easily taught the leading principles of rowing than others; but even those for whom nature has done the most should clearly understand that there is no royal road to a perfect knowledge of the art. Nothing but long continued and properly directed efforts, hard work, and plenty of it, will attain the desired end. And above all things a beginner should recollect the importance of learning to row upon correct principles, since to unlearn bad habits, once acquired, is a more difficult and far more ungracious task than mastering all the principles of the art if properly taught. Again, as an oarsman's form depends entirely upon the manner in which he has been originally instructed and upon his teacher, it is indispensable that those who desire to row correctly should have a capable instructor, and in his absence should ascertain by reading and observation the primary steps to be taken to ensure a correct style and proper form.

It may, therefore, be laid down as a rule that the first lessons in rowing should not be given in the light racing boats of the day; but in a craft so steady that the beginner should be perfectly at ease as to his safety and keeping his balance; it may be an old-fashioned gig, not outrigged, or a skiff. Care must be taken that his seat, mat, or cushion, stretcher, thowl, and oar, are in order and according to rule. If any of these things are the reverse—stretcher too long or too short, thowl worn away—much mischief may ensue. It must be taken for granted that a boat with fixed seats only is used: the sliding seat must be strictly prohibited; and it is desirable to dispense with straps—indeed they are seldom fixed to an old-fashioned boat. The pupil should be placed upon the stroke-thwart, close under the observation and within reach of his teacher, who should sit upon the coxswain's thwart, with the yoke-lines in his hand, or perhaps with an oar or scull instead, by the use of which he can guide the boat better than with lines. The earliest point that should be impressed upon the pupil's attention is the taking up a correct position, for upon this depends future form, whether good or bad. It is scarcely necessary to recapitulate *seriatim* the details of this position, as they are fully and clearly laid down in Chapter IV., and if the instructor does not know them by heart, and cannot practically impart them, he is no teacher. It will be sufficient to mention that the pupil should sit upright and square on his seat, but not too near the edge of it, because, if so, the chances are that the lower part of the back will not be straight; moreover if his seat is not firm he cannot balance the boat. He should sit about three-quarters of the seat aft, that is to say, about $1\frac{1}{2}$ or 2 inches from the after edge, or that nearest his stretcher. Again, he should not sit in the centre of the boat, because the oar, when of a proper length in-board, will just reach beyond the outer gunwale, and to hold it firmly and securely he must be exactly before the handle, and consequently close up to the side of the boat opposite to his rowlock. His feet should be firmly pressed against the stretcher, which should be as short as possible, compatibly with clearing the knees and doing the work in an easy manner, and with perfect control over the oar, the heels close together, and the toes wide apart. His oar should be held with the outer hand close to the end of it, the inner hand from $1\frac{1}{2}$ to $2\frac{1}{2}$ inches off, as already stated. He must then be told to reach out—keeping his arms straight, his body and shoulders square, head up, chest out, and knees apart—and to take a stroke, his instructor not only minutely explaining every separate action and the manner in which it should be performed, but also *showing him how to do it*. The oar must invariably enter the water with the back at least at right-angles to it, although it is naturally somewhat difficult to get a raw recruit to lay hold of the water with the blade of his oar in a perfectly correct position. He must next endeavour to pull the stroke through with the edges of his oar vertical—pressing against the stretcher with his feet, and bringing the weight of his body to bear—and then to finish the stroke as steadily as he can, being careful to avoid flirting the oar out of the water, or winding up with a jerk. There is no necessity to teach him to feather at first, as it is of the greatest importance to instil into his mind an idea of getting a firm, square drag through the water, and of bringing the oar out square, yet meanwhile keeping himself as upright as possible. He must be taught to maintain command over his oar from the beginning, as it too often happens that the oar and not the man is master, and for this purpose great care should be taken that his seat is high enough. This elementary lesson should last, at intervals, until the pupil has gained a knowledge of what he is required to do and how to do it; and the more easily to impart shape, he may be told to unship his oar, and to swing his body backwards and forwards, unaccompanied by the oar—yet at the same time going through the usual evolutions with his arms and legs, as if he were actually handling it. Occasionally he may change places with his coach, and sitting down on the after-thwart watch minutely the mode in which the oar is used by the latter, and then returning to his place endeavour to put the same into practice; and if the boat selected for the initiatory lessons is a wide, roomy skiff, the teacher may now and again sit on the same thwart with his pupil—between the latter and the rowlock—the more readily with his own hands to put straight any inaccuracies of arms, elbows, back, knees, or feet. The pupil should then be shifted to the bow thwart, and be taught to go through the same performance with the bow-side oar. Having satisfactorily accomplished this, he may be taught to feather. When, from simply pulling by himself, he has quite mastered the essential point of rowing an oar horizontally through the water, the next thing is to put a good oarsman into the boat to row stroke, the learner taking the bow-oar as before. It is as well for the teacher to continue to steer—of course now using the yoke-lines—as he can the better watch every movement of his pupil; for if the former row the stroke-oar, he cannot by any possibility pay proper attention to his own rowing, which is supposed to be copied, and at the same time watch his bow-man. The novice will next be taught to keep time and stroke with his model, rowing at a steady, even pace, with frequent breaks for rest; and with this example constantly before his eyes he will make rapid improvement, and should, as he progresses, be further instructed in all the various manœuvres which compose the science: of course, until he can row a fair oar, and in proper form, he will be confined to a pair-oared old-fashioned craft. During these lessons the instructor must be beyond measure careful to teach kindly and considerately, intelligibly explaining any matter not perfectly apprehended by his pupil, and *never losing his temper!*

When considered sufficiently advanced in knowledge, the pupil may be put into an outrigged pair-oared gig, if at hand, or into a four-oared gig or tub-boat, though not with other recruits as unpolished as himself, but with companions of known capability; and he should be shifted from bow to No. 2, and back again, until *able to row equally well on both sides*, otherwise he will be but an addition to the ranks of those men who can only row on one side—owing to the mischievous way in which they have been originally taught—and of whom there are many. From the four he will, in due time, get promoted into the gig eight; but the first racing outrigger he enters should be an eight, as the latter is far steadier and easier to row than a four-oared outrigger, to say nothing of its greater weight, which, under the circumstances, is a desideratum. Of course he will be as closely as possible looked after by his coach in one as in the other, but necessarily less so in an eight than in any other boat.

In introducing a beginner to the sliding seat, it is advisable to impress upon him the fact that his rowing must conform in every respect to the same rules as on a fixed seat, and that he must on no account favour sliding to the neglect of the cardinal principles of catch, grip, and the application of weight. The stroke must be rowed as on a stationary seat, with a full forward reach, an instantaneous catch and application of power—lifting the body, as it were, off the seat, without a thought of sliding—the pupil meanwhile sitting as if on an egg without breaking it; and when his body reaches the perpendicular, the slide will go back without forcing or effort, almost without volition, and the stroke will conclude as before. The legs should press rigidly against the stretcher, and continuously; but above all things the beginner should avoid spasmodic action with them; he should never attempt to kick his stretcher, for, independently of kicking being the cause of numerous faults, it forces the sliding seat back before the proper power of the body is fully applied, and so renders the rowing of the pupil ineffective, and upsets the homogeneous work of the crew. The length of slide for beginners varies under different instructors, from 3in. upwards, but although no hard and fast rule can be laid down, it is far better to begin with a reduced slide, shortening it with stops until the pupil has mastered its elements, and then increasing it gradually to its fullest extent.

With regard to coaching recruits, it must not be expected that the same strictness and attention to rule will be necessary as in the case of selected crews preparing for races, of whom the succeeding chapter will fully treat; still, a great deal depends upon a proper supervision of their work on their entry, as it were, into harness. It will not be advisable to place more than one or two such in an eight, the remaining part of which should be composed, as far as practicable, of men of experience and acknowledged ability, though not, perhaps, of the highest order: the stroke oarsman, however, should be the best that can be conveniently obtained. Long rows, without stoppages, are by no means desirable at this stage, because men unaccustomed to the work soon get tired, and, when weary or distressed, will resort to every expedient to spare themselves, and possibly thereby contract faults all but, if not quite, ineradicable. This is not our purpose at all; what is really wanted is to teach them to swing and to work simultaneously and uniformly with other men. Steadiness, length, and slowness of stroke — in fact, mere paddling — are the means by which alone this end can be attained; and the crew should be frequently stopped during this practice, so as to give rest and wind, and in order to explain and remedy any error observed by the coach. This personage must studiously avoid abusing or bullying his oarsmen, and he should frequently run or ride along the bank, putting someone else at the lines, so

TEACHING BEGINNERS.

as to regard his pupils from every point of view, and to enable him to detect faults which are indistinguishable from the after-thwart. Notwithstanding all this, there is no place like a steady pair-oared boat for minutely supervising minor details of work, and for teaching certain things, but it should be combined with the eight, as men cannot swing in a pair, and must check themselves going back; again, the position of the feet will be different. When form has been learnt, but not till then, a full application of strength and speed may be allowed. After a time it will be readily seen from this desultory practice who are promising oarsmen, and, as occasion requires, and as they approach the necessary standard, they will be promoted to higher positions.

Next, as to scullers. As in the case of learning to row with one oar, the beginner will do well to take his early lessons in a wide, roomy boat, such as a skiff, or old-fashioned gig; a skiff is best, because its leverage is greater than that of an old-fashioned gig. No straps or sliding seats are to be used. At first it is advisable to have some one at the lines to guide the boat and to coach—an amateur sculler, or a waterman may occupy the post. When the pupil is sufficiently advanced, an out-rigged gig, or funny may be tried, After having in this way acquired the knack of holding the sculls and balancing himself according to rule. he can then be put into a wager boat, his instructor rowing in another boat alongside; or, if a double sculling boat is procurable, the instructor may occupy the bow, and the learner the after seat. By this plan the former can steady the boat and guide it, while the latter can concentrate his attention in acquiring a correct seat and a proper method of using the sculls, under the eye and advice of his teacher. The single scull wager boat can subsequently be resorted to with more confidence. The actions in sculling are, for the most part, the same as in rowing an oar. When starting a sculling boat away from a boatyard, the accepted rule is to put her sideways, not end on, into the water, with her head against the stream or tide; the inside outrigger is then held by an attendant whilst the sculler embarks, taking his outside scull and placing the handle through the rowlock from outside, and drawing it inboard until the button is within the thowls. The inside scull is shipped in the same way. The sculler being settled and ready to go, the attendant should take the blade of the inshore scull in his hand, and, keeping it down close to the level of the water, push it gradually out, and with it the sculler and his outrigger together. The boat's nose can also frequently be sheered out sufficiently to get a pull with the inside hand, by backing or holding water with the outer one, when her head is up-stream or against the tide. In coming in at a landing-place, the boat is easily brought up alongside, by holding water with the inside, and pulling the outside scull; but, if coming down with stream, her head must previously be turned round and put up against it, as at starting. The sculls, when not in use, should invariably lie flat on the water, to balance the boat.

In steering, perhaps the best way is to turn the head to the left, though some scullers prefer to turn it to the right, and then the left eye not only catches sight of any obstruction or impediment in the course, but also notices the shadow of objects some distance ahead, the exact nature of which cannot at once be discovered; custom, however, is after all the best guide.

CHAPTER VIII.

COACHING FOR RACES, AND SELECTION OF CREWS.

THE preliminary step in making up a crew for a race is to select the men who are to compose it, and in this particular the most consummate judgment and knowledge are all in all, for everything depends upon the person whose duty it becomes to choose no less than to coach them. This individual, who is seldom or never the regular coxswain, is usually an oarsman of experience, chosen from amongst and by the men themselves; but the responsibility that rests upon his shoulders is immense. He should be a thorough oarsman, and as such familiar with every detail of the art of rowing. He should, if possible, have some knowledge of the construction of boats, the better to enable him to inspect the fittings of such craft as are used, and if not to make trifling repairs, at any rate to extemporise shifts and expedients in critical or unlooked for situations. It must not be supposed that his work is confined to supervising the men's pulling; on the contrary, he is their physical trainer as well as their teacher of rowing, and therefore he should be conversant with the laws of health, particularly as regards exercise and diet. In habits and speech he should be temperate; as thorough a master of his temper as of his oar; firm in exacting obedience to his directions, and yet considerate of faults; most patient, as well as intelligible, in explanation and illustration. One great error that coaches often commit is to suppose that their labours are over as soon as their men get out of the eight: now, many faults in rowing are so subtle that it is impossible to find them out unless the men are studied in pair.

As far as physical conformation goes in making choice of a crew, tall men are to be preferred to short, well built to thin, and heavy men to light, especially for an eight-oar. The limits of weight, which should not be passed without very strong grounds, may be set at 10st. for a minimum, and 12st. 7lb. as a maximum, that is, in condition. The best men will be found to average from 10st. 7lb. to 12st., although there have been many good amateurs, and among them some of our very best, little if at all exceeding 10st. I am now alluding to an eight-oared crew, more especially if engaged in a race over a long distance: for a four, the men and the limits may be much less; but for a pair it is almost a matter of chance what weights come together, though where there is the power of selection, light, quick, active men are to be preferred. No man of less weight than 9st. 10lb., or thereabouts, should be admitted into an eight, if it can by any possibility be avoided without causing detriment to the crew; but it is far better to have a light man who can row, than a heavy one who cannot, and who is so much dead weight to transport. Long bony arms, good back and shoulders, strong legs, and above all things, a powerful, muscular loin (generally accompanied by extreme width at the hips) are desirable qualifications. Yet it is quite possible to have too much muscle, especially about the arms and legs. Other things being equal, care should be taken to have all the crew as nearly alike in height, weight, and build as possible, since the more closely they approximate in these respects, the more nearly alike will they row, and the nearer to the same standard can they all be trained. Their lungs should be healthy and of good size. No man with a flat, narrow, or otherwise defective chest, should be put into a crew. The wind should be good, free from wheezing or cough, the heart healthy, free from palpitation, and not easily excited; but these things can often only be found out after a time.

It frequently happens that the oarsmen put up for selection are ready-made, and do not require much, or in fact any instruction in rudiments; but that they, nevertheless, from the different nurseries in which they have been taught to row, want more or less rounding off and polishing, so as to get them into uniformity. The stroke must first be decided upon, and more discretion must be exercised in his appointment than in that of all the other men put together. Scores of men are able to follow time or stroke with the greatest exactitude, who have no idea whatever of setting it. They are none the less valuable in their proper places, but an accomplished stroke, who possesses first-rate form, great pluck, a good head on his shoulders, and who can maintain the same number of equally well-rowed strokes, whether rapid, medium, or slow, and who when pressed can raise a spurt without hurrying his men or throwing them into disorder—such a man is a pearl of inestimable price. Some men, on the other hand, are so uncertain, and so frequently shift their time and stroke, that no crew can keep together and row steadily behind them. A well tried man is also indispensable at No. 7, to take up the stroke duly. The remainder of the crew must be picked after repeated trials, and after being moved backwards and forwards from one place to another in the eight. It is impossible to write down the exact difference which renders one man more eligible than another; this must be left to the knowledge and discretion of the coach, but if two men are pretty much alike in every other respect, preference should be given to him who does his work in the easiest and most commanding manner. After a crew has been to all intents and purposes finally decided upon, it is not unusual to find faults develop themselves as practice proceeds—to say nothing of breaks-down through sickness — and an occasional change, in consequence, cannot be prevented.

In selecting a steersman it is not a bad plan for the coach to take the crew to one end of a straight reach of water, then to get the boat pointed perfectly straight on some plainly visible object, and to tell the coxswain to steer directly at it: the coach of course will stand still at the starting-place to see if a true course is kept. Few coxswains will do it well.

In allotting to the men their respective places in the boat, it will be essential to be guided chiefly, but not entirely, by their weight. The heaviest men should be located near the centre, at Nos. 3, 4, 5, and 6—especially at 4 and 5—and the weight should be so distributed as to make both sides of the boat equal, in order that she may be evenly trimmed. The after part of the boat should also be fairly weighted with the fore part, to enable her to ride evenly, otherwise her bows will be depressed, and, in boating phraseology, she will "be by the head," or else her stern will drag, and her way be checked; and it is as well to remember that the coxswain adds to the weight in the stern of the boat, and that the fact of shifting his seat a little forwards or backwards will cause a difference. Another point also that should be attended to is the placing the oarsmen on either side so that the four stroke-side equalise the four bow-side oars. It will likewise form part of the coach's duty to pay strict attention to the state of the boat when ashore, to take care that everyone's stretcher is of the proper length and securely fastened, the seats of the correct height, the outriggers unbent and screwed up tight, the rowlocks true, and the thowls, especially those rowed against, in the proper position, and the oars neither sprung nor warped; in fact, he cannot look after his boat too much or too carefully, especially on a race-day. During the earlier part of the practice his proper place is on the coxswain's thwart, where he has all the men within his ken; and it is usual for him to stand up, for he can by that means more readily distinguish the actions and form of every oarsman; but it is more difficult to judge of the time and stroke kept throughout—though not of body faults—when standing than when sitting; and a crew often appear to anyone standing at the lines to be rowing very well together, but the instant he reseats himself he will discover that the time is anything but good. He should frequently accompany the eight on the bank—by far the best place for coaching—putting the regular coxswain, or some other experienced hand, at the yoke-lines; for errors which might pass muster when viewed from abaft, stand out in full relief when seen from alongside, in front, or from a spot ten or twenty yards astern, off the quarter. It is also a very good plan to row behind each of the men, for he can thus detect the true cause of many faults—in most cases, a bad seat in the boat; perhaps without doing this he cannot thoroughly coach his men, because he has not seen them in every possible position. He must use every endeavour to rectify, while in the practice-boat, the smallest fault he may discover; but should his efforts prove unavailing, he will be obliged to take the offending man out in a pair-oared gig after his return from a row with the crew, or before his next embarkation in the eight, and insist upon its being remedied at once. The main point, however, to be *first* brought about is the getting the crew to *row well*, commencing and finishing their work honestly and without shirking. This desirable end is by no means to be compassed at once or in a hurry; and the men will not have attained the qualifications which constitute a perfect crew until after a lengthy probation and constant repetitions of the same lessons, no matter how good they may be individually.

To commence work, the men having been told off,

the coach should take them out for practice in an eight; this boat ought to be a tub or gig-eight. Sitting down upon the coxswain's thwart, he will tell them, when satisfied that they are all ready, to row on. He need not be very critical at first, because, if they are strangers to one another—as far as rowing together is concerned—the boat cannot be otherwise than unsteady, and lurches will be by no means few or far between. It will be sufficient to let them alone for a mile or two, merely causing them to keep a long, easy stroke, and to row as steadily as they can under the circumstances; no bullying is permissible, because at such an early stage, before the men have got accustomed to their seats and oars, much fault-finding will of a surety disgust them; at the same time, a word or two of caution may be addressed to the worst and most careless performers, when they need it. The boat may be stopped after a mile or a mile and a half has been completed, for a brief rest and for shifting any of the paraphernalia which may not be quite shipshape. The row should then be continued, with a short stoppage or even a few minutes' run ashore, when about to turn back, until several miles (out and home) have been covered: the coming in of the crew will then be very different to their going out.

Before embarking in the eight the next day, it it will be just as well for the stroke and No. 7 to go out in a pair-oared gig with their trainer, occasionally varied by a row together in a pair-oared wager-boat, for the purpose of assimilating their rowing as much as possible; and the remainder of the crew ought to be daily taken out in a gig, one after the other, with either the stroke or No. 7, during the earlier portion of their preparation, so as to bring them all as far as possible up to the standard of their stroke; and for No. 7 to be a counterpart of No. 8 is no less desirable than necessary. The stroke will take out the bow-side and No. 7 the stroke-side oarsmen. The latter (No. 7) will, of course, row stroke on the bow side, and it will be just as well to have two gigs put aside for this purpose, as two lessons can be going on at the same time. These lessons in pairs should be repeated day by day until the coach is satisfied that they are no longer requisite.

It now becomes necessary to say a few words upon the rules to be observed by the oarsmen themselves. They must do their work willingly and with a good grace, paying marked attention to the advice offered them by their coach, and giving it a careful consideration on proceeding to put it into practice. Each man, when pulling, should fix his eyes on the back of the man in front of him, in order to keep time accurately. Now, there are two kinds of time, viz., the time of the oars, and the time of the bodies. The first may be acquired by watching the after oar, but in order to get the second, every one must study the man in front of him, and try to perform each individual action and motion at the same instant. Time consists in an immense number of movements taking place precisely at the same moment, and can only be brought about by fixing the attention on one particular person, and by performing each action contemporaneously: this is the reason why No. 7 is such an important place in an eight-oar. A conscientious attention to his own work is required of every man; and when told of a fault by his coach, and ordered to remedy it, the point should be retained in mind and be acted up to. Unless this is done, there is every probability of a recurrence of the error, after a brief interval. The advice I once heard a well-known amateur on the Thames, who was coaching an eight, give to an oarsman who persisted in his fault—more perhaps from carelessness than obstinacy—was much to the point. After repeated expostulations and explanation, he at last said: "Think of it, sir! think of it; and bring your mind to bear as you row each stroke." This is exactly what every handler of an oar ought to do.

During the earlier period of training the work which the crew will be called upon to undergo will be long, steady pulling, over long journeys, say from eight to fifteen miles. The rate of stroke, which should not be exceeded, varies from twenty-eight to thirty-two to the minute, and this will be found quite quick enough, if every stroke is begun at the proper time and fairly rowed out. The same pace should be maintained throughout each day's practice, without quickening or slackening at all. To be well together, every oar must enter and leave the water at the same moment, each stroke being rowed through equally by all. Every back must rise, swing, and fall at the same instant; all the oars must catch the water at one and the same time; they must all be rowed through the water at the same depth, all be feathered and carried on the feather to each succeeding stroke so simultaneously as to appear but as one pair of oars, or even as a pair of sculls; and if they all get hold of the water fairly and at once, the peculiar noise appertaining to this catch, which is like the sound produced by a stone falling perpendicularly into the water, after being thrown up into the air—a rotten egg, as it is called—will be distinctly audible some distance off, and the rattle of the oars in their rowlocks, and the rush of the water aft off the blades, will each be blended into one. The coach should pay particular attention to any oarsman whose faults he may have endeavoured to remedy in the pairs, for fear he should revert to them, and he must impress upon all his crew the necessity of *not rowing a single stroke carelessly*. After several weeks of this practice, and about three weeks or a month before the day of the match, the pace may be quickened and regular racing work commenced, the equivalent of the racecourse being gone over every day. The number of strokes in the minute may be increased up to thirty-two or thirty-four, but it will be found no easy matter to row a quick stroke in a heavy tub-boat. Therefore, if the progress made by the crew is satisfactory, and they have got well together, a regular racing outrigger may be substituted for the tub, but even then thirty-four strokes to the minute will be ample. Great care is required at this point, as the change of boat is occasionally accompanied by a change of style, in a greater or less degree, and individual quickening on, or cutting short, the stroke must be carefully guarded against. Formal starts, as in a race, should after a while commence the quick row—the coach, when satisfied that the men are prepared, asking them if they are all ready, and if not answered, giving them the word "Go." This gives the men confidence, and, moreover, it accustoms them to get a boat rapidly under way from a state of repose, without catching crabs or making mistakes. During this latter period, the regular coxswain should be in the eight, and the coach alongside on foot, or perhaps on horseback; but running is to be preferred, especially if there are gates to pass through, or many men on the bank, for then *the eye need not be taken off the boat*—the great secret in coaching. The coxswain may regularly take the time occupied in the row, so as to compare one day's work with another; but the conditions of wind and water vary so much and so frequently that, except in the most experienced hands, time is, as a rule, the most delusive of all guides. This state of things may continue until two or three days before the race, when the crew may be eased in their work so as to gather a little extra strength, and an increase in weight of a pound or two per man is not to their disadvantage. On the day preceding the race, one row, and that a short one—say a mile and a half out, and the same distance back—will be all that is necessary, and this may be spent in practising starts at top speed, easing up after a hundred or a hundred and fifty yards. The rate of stroke may be increased during the last week to thirty-six and thirty-eight per minute, and the number compassed in the starts will sometimes be as many as forty; but, for rowing the course through, thirty-seven are plenty. On the day of the race it is not advisable to get into the boat before the hour fixed for starting, though it is occasionally done.

The Metropolitan is the only long course now rowed by eights, viz., from Putney to Mortlake, on the occasion of the annual match between the Universities of Oxford and Cambridge at Easter; but the usual length of racecourses for eight oars, and all other descriptions of boats, varies from $1\frac{1}{4}$ to $2\frac{3}{4}$ miles. As a rule, therefore, it will not be necessary for eights and fours, when training, to row sharply over a much longer distance than the course actually to be contested. At the same time, it is sound policy to go over a greater scope of ground, though at a steady, well-defined stroke.

The coaching of a four—a somewhat more delicate machine, and therefore requiring greater nicety—will be much the same as that already described; but it frequently, though by no means necessarily, happens that a four is made up of a portion of an eight-oared crew in training for races at one and the same regatta, and requires nothing more than practice. And now that they row without coxswains, there is all the more necessity for strictness on the part of the coach who is ashore, as there is no one at the after end of the boat to steady them and point out errors, hitherto more palpable to the occupant of the coxswain's thwart than to anyone else. The oarsman who steers by his feet, and is generally in the fore part of the boat, is usually the captain of the crew and gives the orders.

Pair-oared rowing is perhaps the perfection of the art, and it is without question the most difficult mode of oarsmanship. The vagaries described by a couple of badly matched men in a pair-oar are as amusing as they are absurd: this is chiefly owing to inability to steer, and want of practice. In these boats, which carry no coxswain, two men row a pair of oars, as the term implies, the stroke oar being on the larboard, or proper stroke side, and the bow oar on the starboard, or proper bow side. The bow-man is usually the responsible individual, as he not only steers, by means of the mechanical apparatus connected with the rudder, but directs the stroke what to do; and the duty of the stroke is to keep on rowing uniformly, but yet to pay the strictest attention to the orders of his bow-man. The latter, it is scarcely necessary to state, should be the more experienced oarsman, and he steers, mainly, by working the rudder with his feet, and sometimes in a lesser degree by easing or increasing the power he applies to his oar as circumstances require, according to the course he is desirous of taking, looking over his shoulder as in sculling: a well-practised sculler, therefore, makes the best possible bow-man in a pair. If he finds that he cannot get his boat's head round quickly enough, he can still tell the stroke to row easy—but not to stop rowing, as such a course of proceeding would most probably culminate in a capsize—and lay out himself accordingly. More practice is required in this branch of the sport than in any other—that is to say, to perform well, but plenty of rowing together, coupled with watchfulness and attention on the part of the bow-man, is all that is really wanted; coaching, as with eights and fours, is seldom or never thought of, though occasionally needed. When training for a race, the daily spin should equal, or rather slightly exceed, the course to be gone over, but it will be productive of much benefit to take long, steady rows, and to wind up the practice with the spin in question. A pair should ease up one day before their race. The heaviest man should be placed aft, unless the boat is specially built for a heavy bow-man.

CHAPTER IX.

THE VARIETIES AND CONDUCT OF BOAT RACES.

A BOAT RACE is a comparative trial of the speed at which two or more boats can be driven through the water by their respective crews, rowing over the same course at the same time. It is of essential importance in view of a fair trial of skill, that, in addition to rowing at the same time and place, the conditions of the contest should be identical—the water as fair for one as the other, and the boats of the same class, except in special cases, such as handicaps, in which gigs, or skiffs, and wager-boats sometimes meet.

There is but one generally recognised and standard mode of boat-racing, viz., straightaway breast or level races, as at Henley, Putney, and almost every other locality where the width of the water is sufficient to allow of two or more boats starting abreast and continuing alongside to the conclusion of the course. It is necessarily the fairest and most satisfactory kind of all.

Besides straightaway breast races, there are turning races—seldom adopted in this country, except on salt water, though fashionable in America—in which, owing to the sheet of water rowed upon not being long enough for a straightaway race of average dimensions, or for other reasons, the competing boats row out from the starting point to the far end of the course, and after rounding buoys there placed, return homewards and finish at the starting place. It is, however, at best an objectionable method of racing, for knack in turning, which is really no part of racing proper, sometimes materially influences the result; and when boats of considerable length, such as four-oars, are used, there is great danger of fouling at the turning place. In order to obviate this difficulty as much as possible, each competing boat should have a separate turning buoy, placed a considerable distance apart, and, more than this, it must be imperative upon every boat to turn the same way—say from port to starboard, or left to right, otherwise collisions are all but insured. In America there is a rule to this effect.

In some places, however, such as at Oxford, between Iffley and the Barges, and at Cambridge, between Baitsbite and the upper end of Long Reach, where there is not sufficient room, and where the curves are too sharp for boats to row alongside of one another, bumping and time races are resorted to, but they have their drawbacks. The former are rendered necessary when the number of boats competing is large: the latter, as a rule, take place either as a wind-up, when the boats have all been bumped out but two or three, or else when the entries in themselves are scanty. In the bumping races the boats start one in front of the other, as it were in a sequence, a stated distance intervening between them, and a post being fixed for each to start from. Each boat endeavours to bump or touch the boat in front of it, and when this is accomplished, both the boat bumping and the boat bumped draw on one side, and allow the remainder of the competitors to pass onward. In the eight-oared races the result of a bump is, that in the next race, the two boats concerned, whether making an ordinary bump or bumping over two places, change positions. Bumping over two places results as follows: If out of four boats close together, the two in the middle touch and draw aside, and the last one rowing on overtakes and bumps the first of the quartet, that is called a bump over two places. Excepting in the eight-oared races, the boats bumped are disqualified from further competition. Rowing past a boat is equivalent to bumping it.

In time races the boats start in the same manner as before, from posts a fixed distance apart, and finish at posts separated by a like interval, the endeavour of each being to get to its own post first.

The latter are less objectionable than bumping races, which frequently resolve themselves into efforts to run into one another by a quick start, or by putting on a spurt at sharp corners. The time races, on the other hand, are better tests of merit, as they must be rowed through from beginning to end. In both cases the wash of preceding boats leads to much unsteady rowing, but they are by no means such a true criterion of respective excellence as breast races, for boats which are unsuccessful in bumping their leaders in the college eights, sometimes defeat them in level races on wider water, instances having occurred at the Henley Regatta in 1862, and at King's Lynn in 1865.

Handicaps have come more or less into vogue, but they are only applicable to scullers. There does not seem to be much objection to them, for they hold out encouragement to men who otherwise might never take to handling sculls, and if framed on sound principles, and good men are not too heavily penalised, will often produce first rate sport. The great bane of handicapping is, that competitors of quality are, by reason of their superiority, handicapped out of the race. This is contrary to the intentions of the art, which is supposed to place everyone on equal terms. The plan generally pursued consists in allowing intervals of time between the start of each competitor, according to the capabilities of the men concerned. For instance, A. may be started at the hour, B. two minutes, C. five minutes, and D. ten minutes afterwards, the winner being the competitor who reaches the flag first. This method is infinitely preferable to starting them all together and checking off the handicap as the men pass the winning-post. On the Thames, at Putney, $1\frac{1}{2}$ seconds are considered the equivalent of a length in sculling boats, rowing with the tide; on still waters 2 seconds. In America, handicaps between boats carrying an unequal number of oars are sometimes rowed, the handicap being framed on time, in the proportion of so many seconds per oar, the ordinary allowance being from 3 to 4 seconds per oar per mile, of which an instance has been previously mentioned (*vide* Chapter II., pp. 21 and 22). Single-streak boats allow lap-streak clinker built boats 8 seconds per mile, if equally manned, in the United States.

A regatta is a series of races, each of which is between two or more boats, occurring upon the same or consecutive days. The first regatta that ever took place on the Thames was held in front of Ranelagh Gardens, on the 23rd June, 1775. The public prints of that date spoke of it as an entirely novel species of amusement in England, recently introduced from Venice, and added that it attracted a vast crowd of spectators. The second regatta took place at Oatlands, near Weybridge, then the seat of the Duke of Newcastle, at which the Prince of Wales, the Princess Amelia, and a great number of fashionable personages were present, but the records are silent as to the year. The Henley Regatta was established in 1839, when the Grand Challenge cup was first rowed for; but the first match between the Universities of Oxford and Cambridge came off on the Henley waters as long back as 1829, though, on the next occasion, 1836, the venue was changed to London, but the contest did not become an annual one until 1856. The Wingfield sculls were instituted and first rowed for on the Thames in 1830.

Regattas are usually managed by a body of gentlemen called in one place stewards, and in another the committee. The duties of this board, after electing a secretary, consist in arranging the terms of the various races, and fixing the day or days on which they are to be rowed; in receiving, through the hands of their secretary, the entries and entrance fees of intending competitors; in arranging the programme; in investigating and disposing of any objections made against particular crews or individuals; in considering any proposed alterations in the conduct of the races which the exigences of the moment may render necessary : and in awarding the prizes according to the decision of their umpire and judge, both of whom should be appointed by the committee. It is their province to receive and adjudicate upon any objections that may be made by one competitor against another, and to determine all questions of the eligibility, qualification, or interpretation of the rules of the regatta which they have issued; but they should be careful to avoid entertaining any objections from disqualified or dissatisfied competitors against the decision of the umpire, in cases of fouling or other disobedience to the laws which he is appointed to administer. This is the one thing of all others they should decline to enter into or discuss. It is utterly impossible that a body of committee men, who are mostly ashore or close to the winning-post, can form a correct opinion upon any race if they have not accompanied it, and watched every incident, from the start to the finish. It is to obviate this very difficulty that an umpire is appointed, and his duties are clearly laid down in the Laws of Boat Racing, which will be found in detail in the succeeding chapter.

The executive officers connected with a race or a regatta are the umpire and the judge. The province of the umpire is to follow—generally afloat, and less frequently ashore—the race throughout, and to decide upon fouls, should they occur. If the race is rowed fairly out upon its merits, without accident or collision, his post is not an arduous one; but when fouling—the bane of the rowing match—does unfortunately take place, he must act in accordance with the Laws which he is appointed to administer and his own judgment. If, as sometimes happens, he has to perform the unpleasant task of disqualifying an offender, he should make up his mind at once, carry his judgment into execution, and above all things, abide by it.

At the present day the umpire generally acts as starter, as previously mentioned, and from the moment of giving the word up to the time of passing the winning-post, the race is under his sole charge: this is also the case when an independent starter is appointed, the duties of the latter consisting simply of dismissing the competitors who, from the moment they leave their places at the starting post, are under the jurisdiction of the umpire. The readiest and simplest mode of effecting a start is to inform the competitors that he will ask *once*, "Are you ready?" and that if he receives no reply, for which he will allow a reasonable time to elapse, he will say "Go;" upon which the race will commence. Should any of the men not be prepared when he asks his preliminary question, they should sing out in a loud voice, "No!" After allowing a sufficient time to pass, the umpire should again ask the question, and, upon receiving no answer, should give the word. Of the two monosyllables, "Go," given after asking once only if the men are ready, is much to be preferred to "Off," as the former is easier of utterance in a loud and marked manner, and is more readily caught by the oarsmen or scullers lying at the post. It is the signal on the turf, accompanied by the fall of the flag.

The judge is nominated for the purpose of watching

which of the competing boats passes the post first; and with this view a couple of plainly marked posts—one on each side of the course—should be placed in a conspicuous position, so that he may have a clear and distinct line of sight. A flag on one or both of these posts enables the competitors to distinguish the spot where the race ends. It should be clearly understood that it forms no portion whatever of the judge's duty to offer any opinion upon the merits of a race; he is simply to name the boat which passes his flag first; and he should invariably judge the race by the bows of the boats, and not by their sterns, as has been done before now, even at Henley. Our Transatlantic cousins have a rule compelling a judge to decide by the bow or nose of a boat, in their code of laws. There have been occasions on which the judges' decisions have been openly called in question, and it would not be difficult to mention cases in which, through a mistake, the second boat has been placed first, and the first second. Optical illusions are at the bottom of these mistakes, there can be little doubt, but it might, perhaps, obviate all disputes if an assistant were deputed to aid the judge, placed either alongside him, or on the opposite side of the course. We should seldom hear of a conflict of opinion; and competitors would perhaps be better satisfied.

The majority of the races at amateur regattas, with the exception of Henley, are for presentation prizes, which become the absolute property of the winners, but at some meetings so-called challenge cups are offered, with the condition that they must be won two or three years consecutively by the same club or crew before they can become their absolute property. When this is the case, a row over by a single crew should be considered a win, and the prize should be handed over to them, even supposing there is only one entry—otherwise much injustice is liable to be done. At the same time, it is a question whether these quasi-challenge prizes are not objectionable; and it would perhaps save protests, heart-burnings, &c., if they were at once made permanent challenge or perpetual floating prizes, or else absolutely presented. If the former, a presentation prize of some value should be given to each winner in addition to the challenge cup.

Dead heats should be rowed off after the last race upon the card, or, if the competitors in them are engaged in other races, at such times as are mutually agreed upon, or are appointed by the committee or stewards.

Club races, and matches between crews of different clubs, are arranged and conducted by the committees and officers of those clubs.

Regattas for professional oarsmen and scullers, such as the Thames Regatta at Putney, are subject to the same laws which govern amateurs; but in watermen's matches it is not uncommon to find other rules, now obsolete, specially agreed upon between the parties to the wager, under which the umpire, miscalled the referee, has to act, but the proceeding is a most objectionable one, for many reasons. The only detail in which a departure from the authorised code of laws should take place is in the matter of pilotage, as in the contest for the Wingfield Sculls, in which, unless agreed among the competitors to the contrary, pilot cutters are allowed, under a special regulation passed by the Committee of the Amateur Championship, subsequently to the drawing up of the new code for boat-racing, in 1872. This provision was made with a view of placing University and provincial scullers on a more equal footing with Thames scullers, who were presumed to be familiar with the championship course, and to possess a corresponding advantage over strangers.

The following regulations of Henley Regatta are given *in extenso*, as they show more readily than pages of explanatory directions how a race meeting is conducted :—

GENERAL RULES.

No one shall be eligible to row or steer for a club unless he has been a member of that club for at least two months preceding the regatta. This rule does not apply to colleges or schools.

Any club, crew, or amateur intending to compete for any of the prizes, must give due notice to the Secretary of the Regatta on or before the appointed entrance day. In all cases of entries for eight-oared races a list of not more than eighteen, and in all cases of entries for four-oared races a list of not more than ten names, shall be sent at the time of entrance to the secretary, and from these names the actual crew shall be selected. The names of the captain and secretary of each crew or club entering for any race shall be sent at the time of entrance to the secretary. A copy of the entrance list shall be forwarded by the secretary to the captain and secretary of each club so duly entered, with a list of crews (if required).

No assumed names shall be given to the secretary.

No one shall be allowed to enter twice for the same race.

The secretary of the regatta shall not be permitted to declare any entry, nor to report the state of the entrance list until such list be closed.

Objections to any entry shall be made, in writing, to the secretary of the regatta within seven days from the day of entrance, when the stewards and committee shall investigate the grounds of objection, and decide thereon forthwith.

Entrance money for each boat shall be paid to the secretary at the time of entry (as announced).

A meeting of the stewards and committee shall be held immediately preceding the regatta, at which the captain or secretary of each club or crew entered shall deliver to the secretary of the regatta a list containing the names of the actual crew appointed to contend in the ensuing races, to which list the name of one other member may be added, who may be substituted for any one of the crew in the event of illness or accident, subject to the following rule.

No member of a club shall be allowed to be substituted for another who has already rowed or steered in a heat, nor shall any member of a club be allowed to row or steer with more than one crew in any of the heats for the same cup.

In the event of a dead heat taking place, the same crews shall contend again, after such interval as the stewards and committee may appoint, or the crew refusing shall be adjudged to have lost the heat.

The races shall commence above the island and terminate below the bridge. Length of course, 1 mile, 2 furlongs, 20 poles.

No more than three boats shall be permitted to contend in any heat for any of the prizes.

In the event of there being but one boat entered for any prize, or if more than one enter and all withdraw but one, the crew of the remaining boat must row over the course to become entitled to such prize.

Stations shall be drawn by the stewards and committee in the presence of the competitors or their representatives.

Every eight-oared boat shall carry a coxswain; such coxswain must be an amateur, and shall not steer for more than one club for the same prize. The minimum weight for coxswains shall be 7 stone. Crews averaging $10\frac{1}{2}$ stone and under 11 stone shall carry coxswains of not less than 7 stone. Crews averaging 11 stone, or more, shall carry coxswains of not less than 8 stone. Deficiencies are to be made up by dead weight carried on the coxswain's thwart. Each competitor (including the coxswain) shall attend to be weighed (in rowing costume) at the time and place appointed by the stewards and committee, and his weight then registered by the secretary shall be considered his racing weight during the regatta. Any member of a crew omitting to register his weight shall be disqualified. The dead weight carried (if any) shall be provided by the stewards and committee, and be placed in the boat and removed from it by a person appointed for that purpose.

An umpire shall be chosen by the stewards and committee, and his decision shall be final.

The judge at the winning-post shall be appointed by the umpire, and his decision shall be final.

The prizes shall be delivered at the conclusion of the regatta to their respective winners, who, on receipt of a challenge prize, shall subscribe a document to the following effect:—"We, A. B. C. D., &c., the captain and crew of the ——, and members of the —— Club, having been this day declared to be the winners of the Henley Royal Regatta —— Challenge Cup, and the same having been delivered to us by E. F. G. H. I. K., &c., stewards of the Regatta, do hereby individually and collectively engage to return the same to the stewards on or before the next entrance day in accordance with the conditions of the rules to which also we have subscribed our respective names."

If either or any of the above challenge prizes shall not be contested for three successive years, it or they shall then be applied to such other purpose as the stewards and committee may direct for the benefit of the regatta.

All questions of eligibility, qualification, or interpretation of the rules shall be referred to the stewards and committee, whose decision shall be final.

The stewards and committee shall have power to alter and add to the above rules as they from time to time shall deem expedient.

Laws of Boat Racing complete the above code of

general rules. It may added that, until 1872, it was the custom for holders of prizes at this regatta to take no part in the trial heats, but to row in the final heat only. In deference to public opinion, this rule was abrogated at Henley four years ago, though it continues in force for the Wingfield Sculls at Putney, according to the conditions imposed by the donor of the prize.

The following are the principal race courses in common use:

Cambridge, on the Cam, 1 mile 4 furlongs.
Dublin, on the Liffey, Pigeon House Fort to Ringsend, 1¼ miles.
Ely, Littleport to the Adelaide Bridge, Ely, 2¼ miles.
Eton, various, above and below Windsor.
Henley-on-Thames, Remenham to Henley Bridge, 1 mile 2½ furlongs.
King's Lynn, Eau Brink Cut, 2 miles straight above bridge, and 4 miles straight below bridge.
London, London Bridge to Old Swan, Chelsea, 4 miles 3 furlongs.
  ,,   Westminster to Putney, 5 miles 4 furlongs.
  ,,   Putney to Hammersmith, 1 mile 6 furlongs.
  ,,   Putney to Chiswick, 2 miles 4 furlongs.
  ,,   Putney to Barnes Bridge, 3 miles 6 furlongs.
  ,,   Putney to Ship at Mortlake, 4 miles 2 furlongs.
  ,,   Putney to Kew Bridge, 5 miles 4¾ furlongs.
Newcastle-on-Tyne, High Level Bridge to Waterson's Gates, 1 mile.
  ,, ,, High Level Bridge to Meadow House, 1 mile 6 furlongs.
  ,, ,, High Level Bridge to Armstrong's Crane, 2 miles.
  ,, ,, High Level Bridge to Paradise Quay, West End, 2 miles 4 furlongs.

Newcastle-on-Tyne, High Level Bridge to Scotswood Suspension Bridge, 3 miles 713 yards.
,, ,, High Level Bridge to Lemington Point, 4 miles 4 furlongs.
Oxford, Abingdon Lasher to Nuneham Cottage, 1 mile 4 furlongs.
,, Iffley to the Barges, 1 mile 2 furlongs.

Of the foregoing courses those at Cambridge, Ely, Henley, and Oxford, are against stream; while those at Dublin, King's Lynn, London, and Newcastle are tidal.

CHAPTER X.

The Laws of Boat Racing.

When boat-racing first became fashionable in England fouling was not reprobated as it is now, but appears to have been openly sanctioned in some quarters, though objected to in others. In Mr. MacMichael's book of the Oxford and Cambridge boat races we read that in the first eight-oared race between the Universities in 1829, rowed from Hambledon lock to Henley Bridge, a collision occurred at the bend below Remenham island, and that the race was started afresh in consequence of the foul. We also find that when the eight-oared match between Cambridge University and the Leander Boat Club was rowed on the Thames, from Westminster to Putney, in 1837, it was the custom on the London water to allow fouling, and at the wish of the Leander Club the two London watermen, J. Noulton and J. Parish, who were celebrated rivals in steering, handled the lines of the two eights respectively (because of their proficiency in these tactics); but as the University men wished to discover which was really the best crew, it was agreed that no fouling should be allowed, and the Cambridge crew won cleverly on their merits. In the

THE LAWS OF BOAT RACING. 117

following year, 1838, a return match was rowed on the same terms as before, but resulted in a series of fouls from one end of the course to the other. The Leander crew came in first, but were objected to by Cambridge for fouling, and Mr. Searle, the umpire, decided that the race was void. In 1839, when the third eight-oared match was arranged between Oxford and Cambridge, two of the conditions stipulated for were that "*no fouling*" should be allowed, and that the boats should be "*steered by gentlemen.*" In the same year Henley regatta was established, and under its newly-made rules "all fouling was forbidden." In 1840 the Universities met for the fourth time, and a collision was at one moment imminent, but by mutual forbearance on the part of the amateur coxswains a foul was avoided. At the dinner which succeeded the race, Mr. C. J. Selwyn, one of the umpires—in those days there were two umpires, and a referee — when returning thanks for the usual acknowledgment of their services, congratulated the members of the Universities on the gentlemanly and generous spirit in which the match had been conducted. He mentioned the principles which they always maintained, first that gentlemen should steer; next (which follows from the first) that fouling should be abolished; and, last, that victory should be its own reward. These principles, he added, were firmly established, and he thought the University crews had done enough to entitle them to the gratitude and respect of all admirers of aquatic sports for their action in this respect alone. From 1839, then, as Mr. MacMichael observes, a great improvement took place in the tone prevalent among amateurs of the art of rowing, and races were rowed out on their merits.

The rules of boat racing drawn up by the Universities of Oxford and Cambridge, and the principal boat clubs in London—commonly known as the Henley Rules—governed amateur boat racing for many years, although professional wagers seem to have been conducted on no fixed principle, the arbitrary decision of the referee, as he was then called, representing law and justice, until the practice of soliciting the gratuitous services of amateurs of experience to adjudicate upon these matches came into fashion. The gentlemen thus appealed to lost no time in making it generally known that they would be guided by none but the recognised rules of boat racing applicable to amateurs; and they are entitled to great credit for the manifest improvement which took place in the conduct of watermen's matches in consequence of their proceedings. As if, however, to make confusion worse confounded, the Committee of the old Thames National Regatta drew up a distinct set of rules for the government of the watermen competing at their regatta, so that while one code prevailed among amateurs, another was made applicable to watermen—though both contained a provision against fouling. Other regatta committees were not slow in following the example thus set, by drawing up rules of their own. It was no wonder that educated men were somewhat perplexed as to their proceedings during a closely contested race, still less so in regard to illiterate watermen.

To remedy this unsatisfactory state of things, a

meeting was convened early in 1872 by Mr. J. G. Chambers, secretary of the new Thames Regatta, which had supplanted the defunct Thames National; and on the 20th of March of that year, a congress or council of boating authorities representing the Universities and principal Boat Clubs, met at the London Rowing Club Rooms at Putney, and drew up the new Laws of Boat Racing. Twelve gentlemen were summoned, but eleven only came together, Mr. E. L. Corrie, captain of the Kingston Rowing Club, being unavoidably prevented from attending, but his concurrence in the draft laws was duly obtained. The Oxford University Boat Club was represented by Mr. George Morrison, who was in the chair, and by Messrs. R. W. Risley and R. Lesley (president); the Cambridge University Boat Club, by Messrs. R. Lewis Lloyd and J. H. D. Goldie (president); the Leander Boat Club, by Messrs. W. Wightman Wood (captain), and J. G. Chambers, who acted as secretary to the meeting; and the London Rowing Club, by Messrs. Herbert H. Playford, F. S. Gulston (captain), John Ireland, and E. D. Brickwood.

The council wisely resolved to adhere as far as possible to the text of the laws in force at the time, or the Henley rules, as they were called, and to introduce as few violent changes as possible. The cardinal alteration which they did propose, consisted in enacting (Rule V.) that each boat should keep its own water throughout a race, and that any boat departing from its own water should do so at its peril. The rules previously in force on this head were that any competitor who came into contact with another competitor by crossing into that competitor's water, committed a foul;

but that when a boat had once fairly taken another boat's water by a clear lead of a length, it had a right to keep the water so taken; in other words, that if one boat left its own water and bored another, and a foul resulted from that boring, the boat which was out of its proper water committed a foul, and became subject to the penalty of disqualification for so doing; but that if the boat boring was so lucky, or so clever, as to take the water of its competitor without coming into collision, it was thereafter entitled to the water and course so taken. It was also formerly held that when two boats were racing, and one fairly took another's water by a clear lead, and became entitled to keep the water so taken to the end of the course, yet if the two boats afterwards came into contact while the leading boat remained in the water so taken, the boat whose water had been so taken was in fault; but that if they came into contact by the leading boat departing from the water so taken, the leading boat was to blame. The meaning of this enactment was simply that if two boats were racing and one took the other's water when it had a clear lead, it was thereafter entitled to the water and course so taken; and that if the hindermost boat rowed on to the boat which had taken its water while in that water, even if it stopped in order to be run into, the hindermost boat committed a foul, because from the moment the leading boat took the hindermost boats' water, their courses were exchanged, and the water, which previously belonged to the leading boat, thenceforth became the water of its antagonist; also that if the leading boat returned to the water which no longer belonged to it, and the sternmost boat came up and touched it, the leading, and not the sternmost, boat was in the wrong. All this, it must be owned was, to say the least, confusing, and the council did well to sweep away the whole of the enactments in question, and to substitute the far simpler plan of each boat keeping its own water and course from the beginning to the end of a race, in contradistinction to the old plan of taking water. At the same time it must not be assumed that a quick starter is even now precluded from going in front of an opponent, and from stopping there as long as he can do so without bringing about a collision; but all departure of a competitor from his own water and proper course is taken at the peril of instant disqualification if touched whilst out of his true course—according to the judgment of the umpire—and, therefore, what are called " boring," or " washing " tactics are rendered in the highest degree dangerous, to say nothing of their unsportsmanlike character.

The best points of the Henley and Thames National Rules were also embodied in the new code, together with the addition of several enactments which the practical experience of some of the members of the council suggested, the reasons for which were fully and sufficiently explained by their promoters—for instance the power given to an umpire (Rule IX.) to ignore an accidental touch of oars or sculls which exercises no influence whatever upon the result of a race, although strictly constituting a foul; and the power (Rule X.) to caution a competitor in danger of causing a foul unwittingly.

The appeal to the umpire (under Rule XI.) for the purpose of claiming a foul, can be made either by word of mouth or signal. It is usual, when a foul takes place, for a competitor to hold up his hand—as this action is generally accepted to signify that a foul is claimed—and to go on rowing; but after passing the winning post, he should formally make his claim to the umpire by word of mouth before getting out of his boat. It is seldom that either the person fouling, or the person fouled, stops to appeal to the umpire otherwise than by signal, though it is occasionally done. It is better that they should not do so, as the competitor fouled may after all come in first, and by winning on his merits, save the umpire, who will have noticed the collision, the necessity of deciding a race on a foul. In cases, however, in which a competitor stops to claim a foul, he must complete the whole course before he can be adjudged the winner.

It is enacted in the new code (Rule XII.) that a claim of foul must be made to the judge or the umpire by the competitor himself before getting out of his boat. The corresponding rule in the Thames National Code was a far better one, and ran as follows: "A claim of foul (which must be tendered by the competitor himself, and not by anyone on his behalf) must be made *to the umpire* previously to the man fouled getting out of his boat." At the instance of one or more members of the council who had been in the habit of officiating as umpires at Henley, it was proposed to word the rule so that the claim of foul should be tendered to the judge or the umpire, owing to the necessity which existed on a regatta day at

Henley for the umpire to return to the starting place without accompanying the race to its conclusion. The council divided on the question, and in the result the majority were found to be in favour of inserting "the judge" in the rule. The decision is to be regretted, first because any umpire who neglects to follow out to the end a race in which a foul has occurred, fails in his duty; secondly, because the judge can know nothing about the foul; and thirdly, because, although inserted mainly to meet the case of Henley, the Henley Committee refused to adopt the new laws in their integrity, but subjected them to a course of ill-judged revision in half-a-dozen trivial details.

The rule (XV.) forbidding a boat to accompany a competitor for the purpose of directing his course, or affording him other assistance, places it within the power of the umpire to disqualify a competitor who is accompanied by a boat either for the purpose of giving him an unfair advantage by coaching him, or as is more objectionable, by washing or obstructing an opponent; but in scullers' races, such as the Wingfield Sculls, and in watermen's matches, this rule is abrogated by special enactment or agreement, so as to allow of pilot cutters being used.

The umpire is now enabled (Rules XVI. and XVII.) to order two competitors who are wasting time in trying to get the best of one another in a start by mutual consent, to go within a specified time, and in default of their doing so can compel them to start at a signal given by himself.

The following then are—

THE LAWS OF BOAT RACING,

As settled and approved by the Universities of Oxford and Cambridge, and the Principal Boat Clubs in London, on the 20th of March, 1872.

I. All boat races shall be started in the following manner: The starter, on being satisfied that the competitors are ready, shall give the signal to start.

II. If the starter considers the start false, he shall at once recall the boats to their stations; and any boat refusing to start again shall be disqualified.

III. Any boat not at its post at the time specified, shall be liable to be disqualified by the umpire.

IV. The umpire may act as starter, as he thinks fit; where he does not so act, the starter shall be subject to the control of the umpire.

V. Each boat shall keep its own water throughout the race, and any boat departing from its own water, will do so at its peril.

VI. A boat's own water is its straight course, parallel with those of the other competing boats, from the station assigned to it at starting, to the finish.

THE LAWS OF BOAT RACING. 125

VII. The umpire shall be sole judge of a boat's own water and proper course during the race.

VIII. No fouling whatever shall be allowed; the boat committing a foul shall be disqualified.

IX. It shall be considered a foul when, after the race has commenced, any competitor, by his oar, boat, or person, comes in contact with the oar, boat, or person of another competitor; unless, in the opinion of the umpire, such contact is so slight as not to influence the race.

X. The umpire may, during the race, caution any competitor when in danger of committing a foul.

XI. The umpire, when appealed to, shall decide all questions as to a foul.

XII. A claim of foul must be made to the judge or the umpire by the competitor himself before getting out of his boat.

XIII. In case of a foul, the umpire shall have the power—(*a*) to place the boats—except the boat committing the foul, which is disqualified—in the order in which they come in; (*b*) to order the boats engaged in the race, other than the boat committing the foul, to row over again on the same or another day; (*c*) to re-start the qualified boats from the place where the foul was committed.

XIV. Every boat shall abide by its accidents.

XV. No boat shall be allowed to accompany a competitor for the purpose of directing his course or affording him other assistance. The boat receiving such direction or assistance shall be disqualified at the discretion of the umpire.

XVI. The jurisdiction of the umpire extends over the race, and all matters connected with it, from the time the race is specified to start until its final termination; and his decision in all cases shall be final and without appeal.

XVII. Any competitor refusing to abide by the decision, or to follow the directions of the umpire, shall be disqualified.

XVIII. The umpire, if he thinks proper, may reserve his decision, provided that in every case such decision be given on the day of the race.

To the foregoing code, which has been universally adopted in America, the boating clubs of the United States have added two more rules, numbering them 18 and 19, the rule as to the reservation of the umpire's decision standing 20th and, as with us, last:

(a) Boats shall be started by their sterns, and shall have completed their course when the bows reach the finish.

(b) In turning races each competitor shall have a separate turning stake, and shall turn from port to starboard. Any competitor may turn any stake other than his own, but does so at his peril.

CHAPTER XI.

THE QUALIFICATIONS OF AMATEURS.

PERHAPS there is no point upon which so much difference of opinion exists as on an amateur's qualifications, and yet there ought to be no doubt whatever on the subject. In regard to boatmen, watermen, sailors, fishermen, and professionals generally, there is no question.

The word "amateur" is intended to signify an oarsman or sculler who rows for amusement or as a pastime, in opposition to a waterman or professional oarsman who rows as a means of livelihood; but the term is conventionally, and withal somewhat loosely, held to mean a rower who does not compete for money, and a stricter definition is much to be desired.

Amateurs may be divided into two classes, viz.: (1) gentlemen amateurs, and (2) tradesmen amateurs; and although circumstances do occasionally occur in which they compete with one another, it is not desirable that the barriers between clubs of gentlemen amateurs on the one hand, and clubs composed of working tradesmen, or numbering the latter among their members, should be broken down: neither was it ever intended that artizans or mechanics, gaining their living by manual labour, should compete on equal terms with crews composed of members of the Universities, public schools, or principal boat clubs, such as the Leander, Kingston, and London rowing clubs, whatever may be urged to the contrary.

It might have been expected that the Henley Stewards, who are supposed to take the lead in boat-racing legislation, would have drawn up some kind of qualifications for amateurs entitled to row at the leading regatta, but it seems that regatta committees are only too glad to shirk the question, and prefer to deliberate and decide upon the qualifications of individual competitors who are objected to, when protests are actually lodged; and even then they have often great difficulty in drawing the line.

The most recent occasion was in 1874, when a member of an up-river tradesmen's rowing club, who was said to be a tradesman earning his livelihood by manual labour, entered for the Diamond Challenge Sculls. Naturally enough his entry was objected to, and the Henley Committee were forthwith much exercised as to the course they should pursue; but on a full hearing of the case they decided that he was not an amateur qualified to compete at Henley Regatta. This sculler has since rowed a waterman in a match for a stake of money.

Another and still more singular instance occurred at Henley in 1866, when Mr. W. B. Woodgate, who had been amateur champion of the Thames in 1862 and 1864, was objected to as not being an amateur, on the ground that he had rowed a waterman—Thomas Hoare, of Hammersmith—for money, in the spring of the year. The facts of the case were that being desirous of testing his speed against Hoare, Mr. Woodgate arranged to row him from Hammersmith Bridge to Barnes Bridge in sculling boats, Hoare to be paid a sum of money by Mr. Woodgate, if he, Hoare, won, but not otherwise. Mr. Woodgate, of course, rowed for his own amusement, but some heavy bets between himself and a backer of the waterman depended upon the issue. In the result Hoare won. On the objection being handed to them, the Henley Committee, without entering into the merits of the question of rowing a waterman at all, cut the matter short by deciding that as Mr. Woodgate was a member of a *bonâ fide* amateur club—the Kingston Rowing Club—at the time of his entry for the regatta, he was entitled to row as an amateur: the objection was consequently overruled. This decision relieved the regatta committee of all responsibility in the matter, and threw the onus upon the rowing club—the finding being tantamount to saying that so long as the oarsman objected to was allowed by a *bonâ fide* amateur rowing club to continue on its roll of membership, so long would the Henley Committee allow him to row at their regatta. Still there can be no doubt that a man might so act as to forfeit his right to row as an amateur, even though he continued to belong to a *bonâ fide* amateur club; and Mr. Woodgate undoubtedly sailed very close to the wind.

In 1867, at the French Regatta held in Paris during the Exhibition, a four-oared crew from New Brunswick, previously alluded to in Chapter II., rowed against *bonâ fide* gentlemen amateur crews from England and

THE QUALIFICATIONS OF AMATEURS. 131

elsewhere, and won both the races for which they competed. It is doubtful whether the French Committee were aware of the occupation of the members of the St. John's crew, which was that of shipwrights and woodcutters, or they would probably have been debarred from competing, when they were objected to by the London Rowing Club. They might not, it is true, have previously rowed for money, but they are now known to have been working mechanics or artizans, and they were certainly not entitled to row as amateurs. Indeed, within three years afterwards we find them rowing the Tyne crew for a large stake of money, in Canada.

The qualification rules of Henley Regatta enact that for the Grand Challenge Cup for eight-oars, and for the Stewards Challenge Cup for four-oars, any crew composed of members of any University or public school, or of officers of Her Majesty's army or navy, or of members of any amateur club established at least one year previous to the day of entry, shall be eligible to contend. For the Ladies' Challenge Plate for eight-oars, and the Visitor's Challenge Cup for four-oars, the boat clubs of colleges and public schools are alone qualified to contend, and each member of the crew must, at the time of entering, be *bonâ fide* a resident member of such college or school.

For the Thames Challenge Cup for eight-oars the qualifications are the same as for the Grand Challenge Cup, but no crew nor individual member of a crew (other than the coxswain), can enter for this cup and the Grand Challenge or Stewards Cup at the same regatta. For the Wyfold Challenge Cup for four-oars any amateur club or crew is qualified to enter, but no crew or individual member of a crew can row for this cup and the Stewards' Cup at the same regatta. The Silver Goblets for pair oars, and the Diamond Challenge Sculls, are open to all amateurs duly entered for the same.

From these regulations it is clear that officers of Her Majesty's army and navy, and members of the Universities and public schools are undoubtedly qualified to row as amateurs, but for a more precise definition of the words "amateur club" or "amateurs" one searches in vain. The rules are utterly silent on the point.

Now, the committee of the London Amateur Athletic Club, who have had weighty reasons for taking the distinction between amateurs and professionals into careful consideration drew up, in 1866, the following definition of an amateur as a settlement of the question, so far as they were concerned :—

> Any person who has never competed in an open competition, or for public money, or for admission money, or with professionals for a prize, public money, or admission money; nor has ever at any period of his life taught, or assisted in the pursuit of athletic exercises as a means of livelihood, nor is a mechanic, artisan, or labourer.

Again, the Congress of American boating authorities which recently adopted in their integrity the new Laws of boat racing drawn up at the Putney meeting of 1872, issued the following definition of an amateur for general guidance in the United States :—

> An amateur oarsman is one who does not enter in an open competition, or for either a stake, public or admission money, or

THE QUALIFICATIONS OF AMATEURS. 133

entrance fee; or compete with or against a professional for any prize; or who has never taught, pursued, or assisted in the pursuit of athletic exercises as a means of livelihood; or has not been employed in or about boats, or in manual labour on the water.

Taking these authoritative data as a guide, the following will, perhaps, suffice for ordinary purposes :—

Definition of an Amateur.

"An amateur must be an officer of Her Majesty's Army or Navy, or Civil Service, a member of the liberal professions, or of the Universities or public schools, or of any established club not containing mechanics or professionals; or must not have competed in an open competition, or for either a stake, public or admission money, or entrance fee, or with or against a professional for any prize; or have ever taught, pursued, or assisted in the pursuit of athletic exercises of any kind as a means of livelihood, or have ever been employed in or about boats, or in manual labour; or be a mechanic, artizan, or labourer."

In distinguishing between senior and junior oarsmen and scullers, the following regulations have been found to work satisfactorily :—

Definition of a Junior.

"An oarsman is a junior if he—
(a) Has never been a winner of any race except (1) a private match, (2) or one in which the competition was confined to members of one club only, (3) or a race between college

crews, members of the same university, (4) or one in which the construction of the boats was restricted.

(b) And has never been a competitor in any match between the Universities of Oxford and Cambridge, or at the Henley-on-Thames Regatta.

"A sculler is a junior if he—

(a) Has never been a winner of any race except (1) a private match, (2) or one in which the competition was confined to members of one club only, (3) or one in which the construction of the boats was restricted.

(b) And has never been a competitor for the Wingfield or Diamond Challenge Sculls.

"The qualification of a junior oarsman or sculler shall relate to each time of his coming to the starting-post, whether for a trial or final heat.

"In the event of a competitor winning a trial heat for a junior race, and before rowing for the final heat becoming disqualified by winning another race, he shall be entitled to have his entrance money for such junior race returned."

Special cases which do not come within the above definitions of amateurs or junior oarsmen and scullers, respectively, must be referred to the committee of the regatta for decision on their own merits.

CHAPTER XII.

BOAT CLUBS: THEIR ORGANIZATION AND ADMINISTRATION.

ROWING commends itself strongly to the young as a manly exercise and as one of the best promoters of health; but as all young men, and particularly those in *statu pupillari*, cannot afford to purchase boats of their own, and as the sport can be better pursued in company than alone—being essentially a social pastime—the principles of association and combination are resorted to with marked success. By a number of persons uniting and contributing a very moderate sum to a common fund, means are provided for the purchase of boats and their equipments, which would in many cases be beyond the reach of individual members, but which, by a judicious and amicable arrangement of rules and regulations, all can have opportunities of using to their hearts' content. A boat or rowing club is, therefore, an association whose object is to cultivate and gratify a taste for rowing, the members of which systematically contribute a certain subscription for the purchase and maintenance of suitable boats, and all the necessary appliances for the sport, under such regulations as the experience of others and their own wants show to be necessary. Such clubs are generally formed with one of two objects in view—either for the promotion of racing, in which case competition is a vital necessity, or simply for pleasure or exercise; in some cases for all combined.

The history of the early boat clubs is somewhat obscure, even if it be not altogether buried in oblivion. According to tradition there were two clubs of note on the Thames, called the "Star" and the "Arrow" —a six-oared club—in the latter part of the eighteenth century, but they ceased to exist early in the present one, and were merged in the newly formed Leander Club, which adopted a coat of arms containing a star in the upper and an arrow in the lower half, with a hippopotamus for a crest, and "Corpus Leandri spes mea" for a legend. The "Shark" was the great London club of the day in 1815 — in which year rowing is known to have been practised at one University, if not at both—and is believed to have been started before the Leander Club. It is almost impossible to fix the exact date of the establishment of the latter society, though it was probably 1818 or 1819, for Mr. Mac-Michael, alluding, in his Book of the Boat-races, to a proposed contest between the Oxford and Cambridge University crews, in 1837, says, "When it was evident that Oxford did not intend to make a match, Cambridge challenged the Leander Club. This club had been in existence for eighteen or nineteen years, and by its rules was limited to fifteen members. From its commencement it had ranked high, not only as a general crew, but also from the majority of its members having frequently distinguished themselves both in scullers' and oars' matches. Of late years the club had increased so much in celebrity that it was generally considered that nothing on the river could rival its crews in speed. They were the first to patronise and lend a helping hand in bringing out young watermen who showed promise of aquatic fame. It was, therefore, considered a bold, and by some an imprudent, thing for the Cambridge men thus to beard the lion (? hippopotamus) in his den. The match, however, was made, and notwithstanding the prestige of Leander, the betting commenced at 5 to 4 on Cambridge, people thinking that their youth and vigour would win the day against the more matured strength of their opponents, who averaged thirty-six summers." Mr. MacMichael's authority was *Bell's Life.*

The public schools of Eton and Westminster seem to have possessed rowing societies before either of the Universities, for Mr. Blake-Humfrey states, in his "Eton Boating Book," that although the official records of boating at Eton go no further back than 1825, yet rowing was practised there as long ago as 1811—in which year there were a ten-oar and three boats with eight oars—if not for some time previously; and he likewise mentions the fact of Westminster School challenging Eton to row a race in 1820, though no contest took place, the authorities forbidding the match. The Westminster "Water Ledger" which commences in 1813, when St. Peter's College had a six-oar, gives a different date and version of presumably the same affair, as the following extract will show :—
"1818.—The Westminsters were this year challenged

by the Etonians. The race was at length fixed from Westminster to Kew-bridge against the tide, the Etonians refusing to row back." Then follow the names of the crew of the six-oar; after which this note occurs, "the match was put an end to by the positive order of Dr. P——." So that there is documentary evidence extant of a boat club at Westminster School as far back as 1813—perhaps the oldest of which there is authentic record—and of a proposed race with Eton in 1818. In 1816 there is also a note in the Westminster Book showing that there was a Temple six-oared Boat Club on the river Thames; and another note in 1827, to the effect that the Westminster Eight "passed all the club boats on several race nights."

The next clubs of which there is authentic record were at the Universities, and were called the University boat clubs. Nevertheless, as there were college crews and races at Oxford long before 1839, when the Oxford University Boat Club was formally established, it may be assumed that there were also college boat clubs, or what answered the same purpose; but there is no authentic evidence of the fact. According to Mr. Knollys' record of the O. U. B. C. races, the first clubs properly so called appear to have been the College boat clubs of Brasenose and Balliol, whose books commence in 1837, though it is doubtful if the Balliol boat club was formed for some year or two afterwards.

The Cambridge University Boat Club was established, says Mr. MacMichael, between the years 1826 and 1829, for the earliest records of the club contain an account of a meeting held in December, 1828, when a *new* set of rules were drawn up; and the oldest chart of the races is a parchment in possession of the First Trinity boat club, commencing with the races for the Lent term, 1827, which he believes were the earliest college races on the Cam, and from which year he considers the Cambridge University boat club to date.

There was a Guards' Club in 1829, if not in 1824; and the records of Henley from 1839, show that there were many other clubs, such as the Oxford Aquatic Club, and the King's College Club, both of London; the Cambridge Subscription Rooms Club, which won the Grand Challenge Cup in 1841 and 1842; the St. George's Club of London, winners of the Stewards' Cup in 1843; the Etonian Club at Oxford, successful for the G.C.C. in 1844; the original Thames Club of London, winners in 1846; the Royal Chester Rowing Club, winners of the Stewards' Cup in 1855, and the G.C.C. and Ladies' Plate in 1856; the celebrated Argonaut Club, winners of the Visitors' Cup in 1852 and 1853, and of the Stewards' Cup in 1856, in which year the London Rowing Club was formed from the last named Club, with which were amalgamated the Wandle, Thames, St. George's, Meteor, and Petrel Clubs. As it was a vital condition that a club should have been established a twelvemonth before competing in the chief races at Henley, the crew of the new London Rowing Club rowed as members of the Argonaut Club, to which they previously belonged. The Kingston Rowing Club, Radley School, Dublin University, Thames, and other boating clubs swell the list.

With the increased popularity of the sport new boat clubs have been established, not only on the Thames and at the Universities, but at almost every provincial town where there is water to row upon, whether it be a river, the sea, or even a lake or canal. At present it is no exaggeration to say that they may be counted by hundreds; but as it was fifty years ago so it is now—the chief localities at which the sport is practised are Oxford and Cambridge. Every college has a boat club, and the new class of unattached students have formed themselves into boating societies, and put boats on the river. Numbers of schools in different parts of the provinces have now acknowledged rowing as useful, and have inaugurated boat clubs wherever there is a river; and with the increase of the population, and of the towns which that population occupies, fresh crews are constantly in course of formation. The following hints may consequently prove of service to the promoters of such societies, in default of experience of their own.

Boat or rowing clubs have in some cases to be formed *de novo*, and that, too, in places where previously little or no enthusiasm on the subject prevailed, whilst others are started by a secession of members from an existing club,. In every case it is desirable to have a small nucleus of rowing men, past or present, not only because their presence will attract others, but because their advice will be invaluable in establishing the new society. This nucleus having been formed, the next thing is to issue a circular stating the objects of the club, and calling a meeting at some convenient place to consider the subject. This having been done, a secretary, treasurer, and working committee must be appointed, and the latter should be limited at first to five or seven members. When the club is once in working order, the number of the committee can be easily increased, and an efficient captain appointed, who should be selected principally for his knowledge of rowing, as on him will devolve— in the absence of a paid instructor—the duty of teaching the members. As it is usual for each club to have its distinctive ribbon or badge, care should be taken that the pattern agreed upon does not too closely resemble that of any existing club; and in cases of doubt this point may easily be ascertained by applying to the secretaries of a few of the principal clubs, who will most likely be able to give the required information. In fixing on a clubroom, or place of meeting, it is well to have it as near the boathouse as possible; and where this is impracticable, arrangements should be made at the boathouse to enable members to dress, as nothing is more objectionable than for men to loiter about in their rowing clothes after a hard row. As to the annual subscription, it will generally be found that from one to two guineas will be sufficient, according to the number of members, and the accommodation required; but this amount will not by any means cover the expenses of such members as enter at regattas, either as club crews, or as individuals. These extra expenses are generally borne by the competitors; the club supplying the boat, with, in some cases, the addition of the entrance fees. Every encouragement should be given to a crew willing to row in public under the club name and colours, as nothing will so greatly conduce to its prosperity as success in races. A young club can form an estimate of its strength at a provincial regatta before competing at any of the principal meetings on the Thames. The post of captain is one requiring great tact: for the want of it many a promising oarsman has been discouraged at the outset of his rowing career, and his services lost to his club. The secretary, likewise, should possess a thorough knowledge of rowing, but should, beyond all things, be hard-working, and keep the interests of the club at heart. The following will serve for a specimen of the constitution and bye-laws of a rowing club:—

DRAFT RULES.

1. This club shall be called the —— Rowing (or Boat) Club; and the colours shall be ——.

2. The object of this club shall be the encouragement of rowing on the river —— amongst gentlemen amateurs.

3. Any gentleman desirous of becoming a member shall cause a notice in writing, containing his name, occupation, and address, together with the names of his proposer and seconder (both of whom must be members of the club, and personally acquainted with him, and one of whom must be present at the ballot), to be forwarded to the secretary fourteen days prior to the general meeting, at which the candidate shall be balloted for; one black ball in five shall exclude. In the case of neither the proposer nor seconder being able to attend the ballot for a new member, the committee may institute such inquiries as they may deem requisite, and on receipt of satisfactory replies in writing from both proposer and seconder such attendance may be waived, and the election may proceed in the usual manner.

4. The annual subscription shall be ——, due and payable on the 1st February in each year,

5. Subscriptions becoming due on 1st February shall be paid

by 1st April, and subscriptions becoming due after 1st February be paid within two months; or in default, the names of the members whose subscriptions are in arrear may be placed conspicuously in the club-room, with a notice that they are not entitled to the benefits of the club.

6. The name of any member whose subscriptions shall be in arrear twelve months, shall be posted in the club-room as a defaulter, and published in the circular next issued.

7. The proposer of any candidate shall (upon his election) be responsible to the club for the entrance fee and first annual subscription of such candidate.

8. Members wishing to resign shall tender their resignation in writing to the secretary, before 1st February, otherwise they will be liable for the year's subscription; the receipt of such resignation shall be acknowledged by the secretary.

9. The officers of the club shall consist of a **president, vice-president**, captain, and secretary, to be elected by ballot, at the first general meeting in February in each year; the same to be *ex-officio* members of the committee.

10. The captain shall be at liberty, from time to time, to appoint a member of the club to act as his deputy, such appointment to be notified in the club-room.

11. The general management of the club shall be entrusted to a committee of —— members, and —— shall form a quorum; such committee to be chosen by ballot, at the first general meeting in February in each year.

12. A general meeting shall be held in every month, in the club-room, during the rowing season; and at such time and place during the winter as may be selected by the committee.

13. A notice containing the names of candidates for election at the general meeting shall be sent to every member of the club.

14. Any member who shall wilfully or by gross negligence damage any property belonging to the club, shall immediately have the same repaired at his own expense. The question of the damage being or not being accidental, shall be decided by the committee from such evidence as they may be able to obtain.

15. A general meeting shall have power to expel any member from the club who has made himself generally obnoxious; but

no ballot shall be taken until fourteen days' notice shall have been given; one black ball to three white to expel such member. This rule shall not be enforced, except in extraordinary cases, and until the member complained of shall have been requested by the committee to resign.

16. No crew shall contend for any public prize, under the name of the club, without the sanction of the committee. All races for money are strictly prohibited.

17. The committee shall have the management of all club matches.

18. The rules and bye-laws of the club shall be printed, and posted in the club-room, and a copy sent to every member; and any member who shall wilfully persist in the infraction of any such rules or bye-laws shall be liable to be expelled.

19. Any member wishing to propose any alteration in the rules of the club shall give notice in writing to the secretary, two weeks prior to the question being discussed; when, if the motion be seconded, a ballot shall be taken, and to carry the proposed alteration the majority in favour must be two to one.

20. The committee shall have power to make, alter, and repeal bye-laws.

BYE-LAWS.

1. The boats of the club shall be for the general use of the members on all days during the season (Sundays excepted), subject to the following bye-laws:

2. That no visitor be permitted to row in a club boat to the exclusion of a member of the club.

3. That the club day be —— in each week during the season, and the hour of meeting —— ——.

4. That on club days members be selected by the captain (or in his absence by his deputy) to form crews; the members present at the hour of meeting to have priority of claim. Should the decision of the captain or his deputy be considered unsatisfactory by the majority of members present, the matter in dispute shall be settled by lot.

5. All boats shall be returned to the boathouse by ten o'clock at night, except on club days, when club boats taken out before

the usual hour must be returned half an hour before the time fixed for meeting. Any expense incurred by the club through an infringement of this bye-law shall be paid by the member offending.

6. Any dispute as regards rowing in any particular boat or boats shall be settled by lot; this provision having reference more particularly to club days.

7. In the event of there being more members present than can be accommodated in the club boats, it shall be at the discretion of the captain, or his deputy, or of such members of the committee as may be present, to hire extra boats at the expense of the club.

8. The committee shall from time to time appoint one of their number to superintend the management of the boathouse, and to make all necessary arrangements for keeping the boats of the club in a thorough state of repair and cleanliness.

9. All crews sent by the club to contend at a public regatta shall be formed by the captain and two other experienced members to be named by the committee, such crews when formed to be subject to the approval of the committee.

10. In the event of a crew being chosen to contend in any public race or match, such crew shall be provided by the club with a boat for their exclusive use during the time of training; and shall have their entrance fees paid by the club.

11. The expense of conveying boats to public regattas at which crews of the club contend, shall be paid by the crews, but the committee shall have power to repay the whole or any part of such expenses out of the club funds.

12. The committee, on the occasion of a club race or other special event, shall appoint a member of the club to take charge of and conduct all arrangements connected with the same.

13. The member pulling the stroke oar in any club boat shall have command of the crew.

14. Upon the arrival of a crew at the place appointed for stopping, the captain of the boat shall (if required) fix the time for returning; and if any member be absent at the appointed time, the crew shall be at liberty to hire a substitute at the expense of the absentee.

L

15. Every member, on landing from a club boat, shall be bound to assist in housing such boat, and in doing so, shall follow the directions of the captain or other officer.

16. Any member using a private boat without the consent of its owner shall thereby render himself liable to a vote of censure, and, if need be, expulsion.

The foregoing remarks on the formation of boat clubs in cities and towns, are, for obvious reasons, not altogether suitable to colleges and schools; but in cases where they do not apply, no difficulty will be encountered in drawing up a special code, as the secretaries of University and college boat clubs may be applied to with every prospect of a courteous answer to inquiries—perhaps accompanied by a copy of the rules of their respective societies, where such regulations have not been published to the world at large.

CHAPTER XIII.

HISTORICAL RECORDS, A.D. 1715 TO 1838.

THE following miscellaneous memoranda have been collected and arranged as nearly as possible in chronological order, as they are not without interest at the present day, and form perhaps the only combined record of boat racing extant.

The most ancient boat race in the kingdom is the scullers' match for Doggett's coat and badge, rowed annually from London Bridge to Chelsea on the 1st of August—at present on the top of the flood tide, though formerly against the early ebb. The prize was given by the late Mr. Thomas Doggett, comedian, in commemoration of the accession of the House of Brunswick to the throne of England, and consists of a red coat and silver badge, bearing the impress of the White Horse of Hanover, together with several money prizes the product of the liberality of Sir W. Jolliffe and the Fishmongers' Company, who manage the race. It was first rowed for in 1715, but no records have been kept previously to 1791. The competitors were watermen who had not exceeded one year from the date of the conclusion of their apprenticeship, and the number of starters was limited to six, who were drawn by lot from the whole number of scullers who entered. This unsportsmanlike and preposterous arrangement continued until 1873, so that success was no proof of a winner's superiority over all the men of his year, but merely over the other five who were drawn against him. In the year last mentioned the authorities connected with the race resolved to weed out the least capable competitors from the whole entry by letting them all row in trial heats, and by reducing the number by this means to the conventional half dozen. The plan is a commendable one, and winning Doggett's coat and badge is now a proof of some merit, although more than questionable tactics still prevail between the bridges, in so far as washing or impeding competitors is concerned. The trial heats are rowed between Putney and Hammersmith, and the final contest for the half dozen prizes awarded, between London Bridge and Chelsea, in old-fashioned wager boats as mentioned in Chapter II.

Boat racing was in vogue in London, as mentioned in the last chapter, in the latter part of the eighteenth century, and probably much earlier, but with the exception of the list of the winners of Doggett's Coat and Badge, and a note that the first regatta on the Thames was held in front of Ranelagh Gardens on the 23rd June, 1775, no records have been preserved. The feats of the "Star," "Arrow," and "Shark" rowing clubs have faded from the memory of living men, and we are left with the Westminster "Water Ledger" as the first authentic documentary evidence of its practice on the Metropolitan river. This book commences in the year 1813, with a simple list of the crew of the six-oared boat "Fly," viz., Messrs. N. Parry, E. O. Cleaver, E. Parry, W. Markham, W. F. de Ros, and G. Randolph. The "Fly" continued to be the only boat of the school down to 1816 inclusive, in which latter year it "beat the Temple six-oared boat (Mr. Church, stroke) in a race from Johnson's Dock to Westminster Bridge, by half a boat, the latter never having been beat before;" to which is added a note "The Temple boat requested the 'K. S.' to row this short distance, having been completely beat by them in a longer row the same evening." In 1817 there was a new six-oar built for Westminster called the "Defiance," and "sheepskin seats were introduced." In 1818, as already mentioned in the preceding chapter, "the Westminsters were challenged by the Etonians," and a six-oared crew was in course of preparation for the race, but the contest was prohibited. In 1819 an eight-oar, called the "Victory," was launched, but the six-oar "Defiance" appears to have been the representative crew of the school, for there is a note that in the spring of 1821 "the boat improved considerably, and beat the 'Eagle' in a short pull from Battersea to Putney Bridge." In 1823 "a new six-oared cutter was built, and the name of 'Queen Bess' given her in honour of the illustrious foundress. In 1823 this boat's crew started from the Horseferry at half-past five in the morning, and reached Chertsey Bridge by three o'clock. On their way back they dined at Walton, and again reached the Horseferry by a quarter before nine." The crew of the eight-oar "Victory," in the same year, "distinguished themselves in the Temple race and several others." A new eight, called the "Challenge," was launched in 1824, and the record says "this boat did beat every boat that it came alongside of, as also did the 'Victory.'" And again, on the 23rd April, 1825, this boat ("Challenge") started from the Horseferry at four minutes past three o'clock in the morning, reached Sunbury to breakfast at half-past seven, and, after having taken luncheon at the London Stone, just above Staines, went through Windsor Bridge by two o'clock in the afternoon. After having seen Eton, the crew returned to Staines to dinner, and ultimately arrived at the Horseferry, having performed the dis- in twenty-one hours. The locks detained them full three hours, and, including all stoppages, they were detained seven hours. A waterman, of the name of Ellis, steered the boat in this excursion, and both steered and conducted himself remarkably well."

Rowing at Oxford appears to have commenced soon after the beginning of the century, but the accounts are merely traditionary. There were college boats on the river some time before any racing took place. The first known races were those of the College Eights in 1815, when Brasenose was the head boat, and their chief and perhaps only opponent was Jesus. There seems to have been great rivalry between these two colleges, as four-oared races were for some years continually taking place between them. There were three four-oars on the river, one belonging to Brasenose, one to Jesus College, and one to an amateur, named De Ros. In 1820 a race was rowed between the last-mentioned four, and a pair-oar rowed by a Brasenose man and a waterman, in which the four won after a hard race. In 1822 some confusion of opinion arose as to the winner of a race for "head of the river" between Brasenose and Jesus. A bump had taken place, owing to a crab, which for a time delayed the B.N.C. boat, but the race resulted in its coming in first. On a second trial B.N.C. won, but the result of the dispute was that there were no races in the following year. In 1824 there was a four-oared race between Jesus and Brasenose, the latter crew consisting of two B.N.C. men, a Worcester man and a waterman. Both boats appear to have been shut in Iffley lock, and on the Jesus crew refusing to go up-river first, B.N.C. pushed themselves out, and, although hard pressed by Jesus, eventually reached Davis's barge seventy yards in front. The College eights were revived in 1824, when for the last time the contending crews were shut into the lock. The manner of starting was as follows: On the signal being given, the lock gates were opened and the boats scrambled out as best they could. The usual method was for the stroke oar to stand at the bows with a boat-hook, and when the gates were opened, to run down the middle of the boat on a plank or gangway, which separated the rowers on one side from those on the other, jump into his seat, and begin to row: or else the stroke would push the boat out with his hands, going down the side of the boat just inside the gunwale, in which case the crew sat with their oars tossed. Three boats only started, Christ Church, Brasenose, and Exeter, and the latter went head of the river. In the early days the qualification for rowing in a college boat must have been very vague, for in 1823 Christ Church objected to watermen rowing in the B.N.C and Jesus boats. In 1824 watermen ceased to row, but even then a stranger might take an oar, if needed. At this time only four boats could be shut into the lock at once, consequently when in 1825 a large number of colleges put on boats, a new system was devised and the crews took their stations 100ft. apart—the last being just above the lasher. Christ Church defeated Exeter, Worcester, Balliol, and some other colleges not mentioned, and went head of the river, where it remained for many years afterwards.

Eton seems to have been celebrated for its rowing from a very early period, for in 1811 the School possessed a ten-oared boat named the Monarch, three eights—the Dreadnought, Defiance, and Rivals—and two six oars—Mars and Mercury; but although there is no record extant, it is believed that there were boats at Eton very much earlier. About 1812 or 1813, the original Monarch was driven from her moorings by a barge and broken up, but she was replaced by a better ten-oared boat. In these days it was customary to have watermen to row stroke and coach the crews, and the practice continued until 1828, when it was abolished, the captains of the boats rowing stroke. The earliest record of a race is one in 1817, when Mr. Carter's House four rowed against the watermen and beat them; but the professionals had a boat far too small for them. In 1819 Mr. De Ros, frequently alluded to, came from Oxford to Eton with three Christchurch men, in a light four-oared boat, and challenged an Eton eight, but was well beaten. In 1818-20 a challenge passed between Westminster and Eton to row a race, and was accepted, but the authorities prevented the race taking place, and the schools did not meet for some years. Eton, it is said, rowed a quicker stroke than any other crew on the Thames, Westminster especially pulling a very slow one—no doubt from practising on tidal water. From 1825 the official record of Eton boating commences, although races among members of the College had been in vogue from 1823, if not before.

1817. G. Gwyngell, on the 20th September, finished rowing 1000 miles in 20 days.

1820. Mr. Gulston's (Millbank) four-oared match for a silver cup and cover, was won by Mr. T. Hunt's crew, on the 22nd August.

1822. Brocking (? Brooking) beat Noulton, Swan to Swan, against tide, on the 25th November. These men were evidently watermen, and probably rowed from London Bridge to Chelsea.

1824. A six-oared crew of the Guards rowed against time from Oxford to Westminster in $15\frac{1}{4}$ hours, being matched to do the distance within 16 hours. The crew, consisting of Captains Short, Westenra, Douglas, Blane, Hudson, and Standen, all of the Scots Fusilier Guards, left Oxford at 3 a.m., reached Maidenhead at 11h. 3m. a.m., Windsor Bridge at 1 p.m., Teddington at 4h. 30m. p.m., Putney Bridge at 6h., Battersea Bridge at 6h. 30m., and Westminster Bridge at 6h. 45m. p.m., winning by three quarters of an hour, on the 12th May.

1826. At Cambridge eight-oared rowing was not in fashion as soon as at Oxford, for the first eight, belonging to St. John's College and built at Eton, was launched in this year; and the eight-oared races, or as they are now called, the First Division eights, were established and rowed for in 1827, on which occasion Trinity finished head of the river. There were only six boats on the Cam on that occasion, viz., a ten-oar and an eight-oar belonging to Trinity, an eight-oar belonging to St. John's, and three six-oars belonging to Jesus, Caius, and Trinity, Westminster.

1828. Seven gentlemen rowed from Westminster to Oxford and back, in a four-oar, in 69 successive hours. ——Coates completed rowing 1000 miles in 1000 hours in Chelsea reach, on the 8th September.——In the same year Harris beat J. Parish—no doubt in a professional sculler's match.

Eight-oared races having become thoroughly established at Oxford and Cambridge, and the art of rowing gradually increasing in favour at both Universities, the question of a contest between them was not long in suggesting itself. After some trouble in settling the preliminaries, it was arranged in 1828 that representative crews should meet on neutral water at Henley-on-Thames in the following year.

1829. Westminster and Eton were not slow to follow the example—indeed, they may very justly be credited with setting it by their challenge in 1818-20— and consequently the year 1829 is a memorable one in aquatic annals. At a meeting of the Cambridge University Boat Club, held in Lent term, 1829, Mr. Snow, of St. John's, was requested to write to Mr. Staniforth, of Christ Church, Oxford, proposing to make up a University match for the ensuing Easter vacation, at or near London. As rowing at Oxford did not begin until after Easter, it was found impossible to hold the race until the summer. Considerable correspondence passed before it was agreed that the course should be from a point above Hambledon Lock to Henley Bridge, a distance of two and a quarter miles, against stream, and that the race should be rowed on the 10th of June, in the evening. The Cambridge crew, whose colour was pink, won the toss for position, and took the Berkshire side. Before reaching Remenham the Cambridge coxswain fetched out into the stream, as if he desired to pass on the Bucks side of the island, while the Oxford men had made up their minds to pass on the inner or Berkshire side of it, and as the competing boats were not clear of one another at the corner below the eyot, a collision occurred. The eights were ordered to row again, and Oxford won by five or six lengths, though details of the race are not extant. The coxswains were both amateurs, and members of their respective Universities, and Bishop Selwyn rowed No. 7 in the Cambridge crew.——In the following month the first match between Eton and Westminster was rowed, the date being the 27th July, 1829, and the course from Putney to Hammersmith, through the bridge, and back through the centre arch of Putney bridge. Brumwell, of Vauxhall, a professional, steered the Westminster crew, and Honey, of Lambeth, a boatbuilder, guided Eton; the latter won easily.——On the 16th September Mr. C. Newnham's crew defeated Mr. Brown's crew in a four-oared match, starting from Westminster bridge up round Putney bridge, down round Carey's bath (perhaps off the Temple) and up again to Westminster bridge. Mr. Newnham was an amateur, who for many years officiated as referee in watermen's matches on the Thames even up to a very late date, and who, as a witness at the celebrated trial of *Sadler* v. *Smith* in 1868—regarding a disputed boat race—was styled by Sir A. Cockburn, Lord Chief Justice of England, "the Nestor of the Thames."——A record is extant that in this year "the Oxonians beat the club of the Guardsmen in a boat excursion from Oxford to London," but no date or particulars are given.

1830. There was a race between two House eight-oars at Eton, besides the "pulling" or pair-oared, scullers', and punting races.——On the 18th June a London amateur eight-oar beat Oxford, 200*l.* (*sic*).——The Wingfield sculls were presented by Mr. Henry C. Wingfield to the amateur scullers of the Thames, to be held by the best for the time being, on condition of his rowing at half-flood from Westminster to Putney against all challengers, annually, on the 10th day of August for ever. They were won by Mr. J. H. Bayford, who beat Messrs. Lewis, Wood, Horneman, Revell, A. Bayford, C. Duke, and Hume.——In this year Charles Campbell won a purse of sovereigns, but the prize was withheld owing to a dispute. On the 19th August, with J. Williams for a partner, he rowed a pair-oared match against Mitchell and Parish, but the latter won.

1831. Eton and Westminster again met in eight-oars, but at Maidenhead, the course being from the bridge to Queen's Eyot, below Monkey Island, and back, a distance of something like five miles. Eton, steered by a waterman, again won easily.——An eight-oared match was also, according to the Eton book, rowed during this year between the Leander Club and the School, in which the former won, but no date or place is given, though no doubt it was rowed at Eton. This appears to be the first mention of a Leander eight on record.——A scullers' match for the championship of the Thames—the first recorded—was rowed on the 9th September from Westminster to Hammersmith—though in one account it is rendered Westminster to Putney—between Charles Campbell, of Westminster, aged 26 years, weighing 11½ stone, and John Williams, of Waterloo Bridge, and was won by Campbell, who became the first champion, and held the title for something like fifteen years.

1832. There was a match at Eton between the "six" and the "eight," which the latter won.——On the 13th August, John Williams rowed a boat (old-fashioned, of course, for outriggers were not invented) from Waterloo Bridge to Gravesend, back up to Richmond, and down again to Waterloo Bridge in 11½ hours, winning by 1½ hours, 100*l*. to 20*l*. being wagered that he would not do it in 13 hours.

1833. Queen's College is chronicled as head of the river at Oxford, this being the only record between 1825 and 1834. Christchurch, it is true, was said to have kept that position for many years, but the precise number is not given. However, there seems to be no doubt that Christchurch was head in 1834, 1835, and 1836, after which the official record commences.—— On the 24th June, 1833, a regatta took place on the

Thames, off Wandsworth, for a pair of silver cups given by the proprietor of the White Horse tavern, for ten four-oared cutters, and the prize fell to Cox's crew, of Wandsworth. It thus seems evident from the number of boats entered, that four-oared rowing was a common practice on the metropolitan river.

1834. There seems to have been no attempt to get up another race between the Universities till this year, and after all it fell through; 1835 likewise passed without a match.——C. Campbell beat F. Godfrey in a scullers' match on the 27th June—probably for the championship of the Thames.———About this year H. Clasper rowed a four-oared gig match on the Tyne against another North Country boat, and won easily, his crew being composed of W. Clasper, J. Thompson, R. Dinning, H. Clasper (stroke), R. Clasper (coxswain). From this time Clasper's crew appear to have won the principal prizes at a regatta held annually on the Tyne.

1835. The names of two celebrated London watermen appear for the first time, viz., Robert Coombes, of Millbank—a little man who weighed, when in the height of his fame, 8st. 12lb.—and John Phelps, of Fulham. On the 16th July Robert Coombes, then twenty-seven years old, rowed and was third—beaten by W. Watts (1st), John Phelps (2nd)—in a sculler's match from Westminster to Putney; but he beat Voss (4th), J. Kipping (5th), J. Carter (6th), and William Parish (last). He defeated G. Campbell, John Phelps, and Kipping, in a sculler's race from Westminster to Putney on the 12th August, but was beaten by Kipping on the same course on the 27th of the month.————On the 14th September following, John Phelps of Fulham rowed a match with J. Kipping on the usual course and beat him.

1836. The Oxford and Cambridge crews met for the second occasion, but for the first time on London water, on June 7th, the course being from Westminster to Putney, and in the result Cambridge won easily, the coxswains being members of the Universities. Mr. T. S. Egan steered Cambridge for the first time. ————Eton also rowed Westminster at Staines and defeated them. It was previously agreed that no fouling should take place until after a mile had been rowed. Before this distance had been completed, Westminster, who were ahead, tried to prevent Eton passing, and caused a foul. In the scrimmage the Westminster crew had an oar broken, their rudder unshipped, and their boat turned right round. Eton then went in front, but were called back by the umpires, and the race re-started from Staines Bridge, the course being from Staines to Penton Hook and back. Again Westminster took the lead, and again fouled Eton as they came up alongside. The latter got clear, but were again overtaken by Westminster, and another foul ensued. After more fighting Eton got away and won. This contest was considered a very gallant and spirited affair. I need scarcely say that watermen steered both boats.————On the 19th July an annual pair-oared race of the Leander Club was rowed from Vauxhall to Putney, and was won by Messrs. James Layton and Horneman, who beat five other crews. ————Colonel Greenwood and Captain Foley, Grenadier Guards, rowing a pair of oars, beat John and W.

Emery, watermen, on the 29th July, the latter rowing sculls, in a match for 50*l*. a side, from Vauxhall to Putney, the watermen being swamped.

1837. This year witnessed another endeavour to arrange a University race, but it fell through, and Cambridge made a match from Westminster to Putney with the Leander Club instead, and beat them cleverly by seven seconds after a splendid race. The Leander crew was manned by Messrs. Shepheard, James Layton, H. Wood, Lloyd, Sherrard, Dalgleish, Lewis, Horneman or Hornby (stroke), James Parish, the waterman, steering them as usual.——Eton again rowed Westminster, the course being on the Thames, at Datchet, from the Bridge to the New Lock, about a mile and a quarter, and back again, and the date May 4: amateur coxswains steered both eights. In turning at the lower end of the course a foul occurred, and Eton got away first, but Westminster rowed past them, and won by three or four lengths. The King and his suite attended.—— On the 10th June, an eight-oared match was rowed at Henley, from Hambledon to the bridge, between Queen's College, Oxford, and St. John's College, Cambridge, the head boats of the Universities; Queen's College winning easily.——In this year a pair of silver challenge sculls were presented to the Lady Margaret Boat Club, at Cambridge, by Mr., now Sir P. Colquhoun, and were rowed for between Westminster and Putney, being won on the 16th June, by Mr. Berney; but they were subsequently presented by the Lady Margaret Boat Club to the competition of the whole University of Cambridge, in 1842, and have been rowed on the Cam ever since.——On the 21st July, Messrs. J. Layton and Dalgleish won the Leander Club pairs, rowed between Westminster and Putney, beating Messrs. Shepheard and Wood, and Hornby and Lander.——In July also, J. Dodd, J. Phelps, T. Byford, and C. Campbell, Mr. E. Searle, junior (coxswain), beat a Saltash or Plymouth crew in a match from Westminster to Kew.——In September, Mr. George Lander (amateur), with J. Williams (waterman), rowed a pair of oars from Oxford to Westminster Bridge, in 18h. 42min., winning a bet of 100*l*. to 10*l*. laid on time. Shortly before the match Mr. Lander weighed 12st. 7lb., but on going to scale a few days afterwards, only drew 11st. 2lb. Williams also worked like a horse.——The Temple Club declined a challenge from Westminster to row an eight-oared race.

1838. A return match with Cambridge was proposed by the Leander Club on the same terms as before, and was rowed on the 10th June, from Westminster to Putney; but, although the Londoners came in first by a length, there had been so much fouling, contrary to previous agreement, that the umpire declared the race void. The Leander crew were the same as in 1837, except that the stroke had left the crew, and Mr. Bishop entered it. The watermen, Noulton and Parish, again steered.——A match was likewise arranged between Eton and Westminster, but did not come off owing to the non-appearance of the latter crew, part of whom were locked up by the head master, in order to prevent the race taking place. —— Robert Coombes beat John Phelps in a sculling match from Westminster to Putney, on the 26th July, by five lengths; "Honest John" as he was then called, rowing one of the gamest wagers on record, although he was astern from start to finish.

—— In October Coombes beat John Kelley, of Fulham, over the usual course, and challenged C. Campbell for the championship. They met on the 1st November, but the aspirant was unsuccessful, for Campbell won easily.

There is a note in the Trinity College book to the following effect: Rowing had now taken its proper place among the national pastimes, and the want of a central spot for an annual regatta was much felt; and after much discussion, Henley-on-Thames was chosen, and it was decided that a regatta should be held there the following year.

163

CHAPTER XIV.

HISTORICAL RECORDS (*continued*), A. D. 1839
TO 1855.

ROWING now became a thoroughly national sport, conducted on acknowledged and equitable principles—the institution of Henley Regatta in 1839 marking an epoch in the history and management of boat-races. Regattas, many of them amateur and professional combined, began to be held at various places in the United Kingdom, for we find records of a Maidenhead Regatta in 1839, Liverpool Regatta in 1840, Norwich in 1841, Chester, and Manchester-Salford Regatta in 1841, Erith, Newcastle-on-Tyne, and Oxford City in 1843—in which latter year the Thames Regatta was established at Putney,—Nottingham in 1844, Lancaster (Halton Water) and Worcester in 1845, Isleworth, Mortlake, Richmond, and Durham in 1846, Bath in 1847, Cliefden and Maidenhead in 1849, Stockton-on-Tees in 1850, and Talkin Tarn, near Brampton, in Cumberland, in 1851. There were likewise numerous four-oared, pair-oared, and scullers' races among professionals, the chief performers in them—most of whose names are as familiar as household words—figuring from time to time in the watermen's race for a purse

M 2

of sovereigns, which for many years formed not the least interesting feature of the Henley Regattas, until steam, and the improved speed of racing boats, drove the umpires from the watermen's eight into steam launches, capable of running from Remenham to Henley Bridge, against stream, in less than five minutes. It is, therefore, manifestly impossible, within the limits of a chapter such as the present, to give details of, or even to record, from this period any but the most noteworthy occurrences, and even those must be chronicled in the shortest possible manner. This is the less to be regretted, as full particulars of all the Henley Regattas can be obtained in the form of a pamphlet* issued on the spot, and added to from year to year; besides which a boating register† in some degree corresponding to Ruff's Guide to the Turf, published annually in London, and other publications alluded to in this volume, will in a great measure supply the information in more concise form than the pages of *Bell's Life* or the *Field* newspapers.

Early in 1839, then, the good people of Henley-on-Thames set about taking measures for holding a regatta during the summer; funds were collected, and the Grand Challenge Cup for eight-oars was founded. The form which the manufacturers gave it was that of the celebrated Warwick vase.‡ It is supported by a shaft or stem covered with bulrushes, &c.; the figures of

---

* An *Account of the Regatta*, Kinch, publisher, Henley.

† *Rowing Almanack*, Virtue and Co., Ivy-lane, Paternoster-row.

‡ *Vide* Vignette on the cover.

Father Thames with his urn and cornucopia recline on the neck of the cup. The handles are also formed of bulrushes, and spring from heads of Thames and Isis, after those by the Hon. Mrs. Damer on the keystones of Henley Bridge. A large space was left on it for inscriptions, but it is now covered with names inside and out. For this handsome prize six eight-oars entered the lists, five from Oxford, viz., the University Boat Club, Brasenose College (Childe of Hale), Exeter, Wadham, the Oxford Etonian Club, and First Trinity, Cambridge (Black Prince). Some disappointment was felt that neither the Cambridge University Boat Club nor the Leander Club had entered. The O.U.B.C. and Exeter did not start. In the first heat the Etonian Club beat Brasenose; in the second, First Trinity beat Wadham after a good race; and in the deciding heat First Trinity beat the Oxford Etonian Club after a most severe struggle, the crews being nearly level at Poplar Point, whence First Trinity were served by the inside station. The Town Challenge Cup for four-oars was also rowed for.——The Universities of Oxford and Cambridge met for the third time in eights, and rowed from Westminster to Putney, Cambridge winning easily, and the celebrated Mr. Stanley, of Jesus, who was one of the first amateurs to row a long stroke, occupying No. 8 thwart.——The Oxford University Boat Club was formally established this year, and so were the University pair-oars.——In this year also a four-oared match was rowed from Vauxhall to Putney between a crew of officers of the Grenadier Guards, Col. Greenwood stroke, and a crew of officers of the Coldstream Guards, Capt. Drummond stroke, for 500*l.*

a side, in which the Grenadiers won.——A London waterman's crew, composed of G. Campbell, W. Pocock, J. Phelps, and C. Campbell, W. Campbell (coxwain), beat a Clyde crew in a four-oared gig match at Liverpool for 100*l.* a side.

1840. Cambridge beat Oxford, Mr. C. Vialls rowing stroke of the former crew.——The Leander Club won the Grand Challenge Cup at Henley, defeating in the final heat First Trinity, Cambridge, the holders, and five other crews.——A Leander four won the Victoria Cup at Liverpool Regatta, and a Leander six-oar likewise won the Ladies' Cup at the same meeting; at which the Sons of the Thames crew, manned by R. Newell, R. Doubledee, W. Noulton, and R. Coombes, J. Parish (coxswain), won the Champion Purse of 100*l.*, for four-oars, beating the Nymph 'crew of London, composed of J. and H. Maynard, Shelton, J. Doubledee, Simmons (coxswain) and four other crews from Chester, Hull, Cork, and Liverpool.——In this year the Oxford University Boat Club four-oared race was established, and was won by Brasenose College.

1841. Cambridge again beat Oxford, the former, with the Hon. George Denman and the Hon. L. Denman in the crew, rowing in a clinker built, and the latter in a carvel built boat, both constructed by Messrs. Searle. ——At Henley the Cambridge Subscription Rooms crew, with Mr. Justice Brett stroke, the late Lord Justice Selwyn No. 5, won the Grand Challenge Cup from the Leander Club in the final heat by a foul. The Leander coxswain shortly after the start, and before he had a clear lead, bored the Cambridge Rooms' crew, and fouled their oars. The Leander crew came in first, but the umpire awarded the race to their opponents. The Leander Club thereupon challenged the Cambridge crew to row for either 1000*l.* or 500*l.*, or " even for love," but the offers were declined.——A four-oared race for medals was likewise rowed at Henley, in which the Oxford Aquatic Club of London beat the Cambridge Rooms' crew, and St. George's Club of London; in one record this race is said to have been for the New, or Stewards' Cup.——An eight-oared match was, however, soon afterwards arranged and rowed between the Leander Club and the Cambridge Subscription Rooms' crew from Westminster to Putney on the 7th August, which the former won easily.—— The Oxford University Sculls were established. The long stroke, with a sharp catch at the beginning, was this year inculcated at Oxford by Mr. Fletcher Menzies, of University College.——R. Coombes, in a sculling boat, beat two pairs of oars pulled by Clyde men at Greenock Regatta.——A London crew, composed of H. Shelton, R. Newell, and the two Doubledees, J. Parish (coxswain), beat a Southampton crew for the 1000 francs prize for fours at Havre Regatta; and at the same meeting beat eight Frenchmen for 500 francs a side.

1842. Oxford beat Cambridge, the Westminster to Putney course being used for the last time. At Henley the Cambridge Subscription Rooms' crew, who were the holders of the Grand Challenge Cup, beat the Cambridge University crew by 2ft. or 3ft. in the final heat; the latter having beaten the Oxford Aquatic Club in one of the trial heats by a yard. The Stewards'

Cup was established, and was won by the Oxford Aquatic Club of London.——A London crew, composed of R. Newell, the two Doubledees, R. Coombes, J. Parish (coxswain), beat H. Clasper's crew, composed of himself and his three brothers, in a match on the Tyne for 150*l*. a side—this being the race alluded to in Chapter II., p. 12.——Westminster beat Eton from Kew Eyot to Putney Old Bridge.—— Coombes defeated Newell in two scullers' matches between Westminster and Putney, the latter being swamped during the first race.

1843. This was the year of the famous seven-oared race, and it happened at Henley Regatta, as follows: In the first heat for the Grand Challenge Cup, First Trinity, Cambridge, beat the Oxford Aquatic Club crew from London; in the second heat the Oxford University Boat Club crew beat the Oxford Etonian Club; and in the third heat Oxford University beat First Trinity. The deciding heat, therefore, lay between the O.U.B.C. and the Cambridge Subscription Rooms' crew from London, who were the holders of the Cup. The stroke of the Oxford crew, Mr. Fletcher Menzies, had been unwell from the time of leaving the University. He managed to get through the trial heats, but in stepping into his boat to go down to the post for the final heat he fainted. A deputation from the crew thereupon went to the Cambridge Subscription Rooms' crew, and asked if another man might be allowed to fill Mr. Menzies' place. The rules of the Regatta, however, forbade the substitution in the final heat of a man who had not rowed in the trial heats, so there was no help for it, but to withdraw from the race or to adopt the alternative of rowing with seven oars. The latter plan was resolved upon, No. 7 in the Oxford boat being shifted to the stroke thwart, and No. 1 to No. 7—the bow thwart being left vacant. When the deciding heat was rowed off, Oxford held their own from the very first, and clearing themselves before reaching Poplar Point, won easily by upwards of two lengths. The winners, Messrs. ——, 2 R. Menzies, 3 E. Royds, 4 W. Brewster, 5 G. D. Bourne, 6 J. C. Cox, 7 R. Lowndes, G. E. Hughes (stroke), A. Shadwell (coxswain), were one of the heaviest and best eights that up to that time had been seen at Henley. Their boat is a historical one, for it was built by King, of Oxford, the floor being modelled by Mr. F. Menzies, and a great part of the boat actually made by him: after lasting for some years as a kind of sacred model, it was dismembered to form souvenirs such as oars, rudders, and snuff boxes, till at last the portion containing the coxswain's thwart was converted, twenty-five years after its launch, into the Presidential chair for the barge of the O.U.B.C. The St. George's Club won the Stewards' Cup.——The Royal Thames Regatta was established at Putney. The Gold Challenge Cup for eight oars, which was to become the property of the Club that could win it three years in succession, was won by the Oxford University Boat Club, who beat the Oxford Aquatic Club, Leander Club, Cambridge Subscription Rooms, and Civil Engineers' College crews. The Silver Challenge Cup for four-oars was, however, won by the Leander Club. The Champion four-oars were not yet established.

Eton beat Westminster from Putney Bridge to Mortlake Church.——A London four, manned by Newell, T. Goodrum, T. and R. Coombes, D. Coombes (coxswain), beat an eight-oar manned by Frenchmen at Havre Regatta.——The Leander Club won the fours and pairs at Erith Regatta.

1844. At the Royal Thames Regatta, the Oxford University Boat Club beat the Cambridge University Boat Club (2) and the Leander Club (3) for the Gold Challenge Cup. The Leander Club won the Silver Challenge Cup for four-oars. The London four, manned by T. Coombes, J. Phelps, Newell, and R. Coombes, beat the Newcastle four, R. Clasper, E. Hawkes, W. Clasper, and H. Clasper, and three other crews, for the champion prize of 100 sovereigns; but Clasper, who rowed in an outrigger, which he introduced on the Thames for the first time, won the 50l. prize for fours at the same regatta.——The Diamond Sculls were established at Henley, and were won by Mr. T. Bumpstead, of London. The Oxford Etonian Club won the Grand Challenge Cup, and the O.U.B.C the Stewards' Cup.——R. Coombes beat H. Clasper in a sculling match on the Tyne.—— The University Pair Oars — called the Magdalene Silver Oars—were established at Cambridge.

1845. Cambridge beat Oxford from Putney Bridge to Mortlake Church : Putney course first used.—— At Henley Regatta the Cambridge University Boat Club beat Oxford University—these being the only two competitors—for the Grand Challenge Cup.——The Ladies' Challenge Plate for eight-oars was established, and won by the St. George's Club, of London. The

O.U.B.C. won the Stewards' Cup after an exciting race with the St. George's Club. The judge at the bridge considered it a dead heat, but the umpire awarded the race to the Oxford boat. The pair-oared race for Silver Wherries—now known as the Silver Goblets —was established, and won by Messrs. Arnold and Mann, of Cambridge.——Westminster beat Eton.—— At the Royal Thames Regatta the Cambridge Subscription Rooms won the Gold Challenge Cup from the Oxford University Boat Club, Neptune, and St. George's Clubs. The O.U.B.C. beat the St. George's Club (crews same as at Henley) for the four-oared cup. The Champion Fours, for watermen, was won by Clasper's crew, manned as in 1844, Coombes's crew being second.——Clasper beat W. Pocock in a sculler's match on the Tyne.——The Leander Club won a Silver Presentation Cup, value 70*l*. at Erith Regatta.

1846. Cambridge beat Oxford, Mortlake Brewery to Putney. This was the first University match rowed in outriggers.——At Henley the Thames Club won the Grand Challenge Cup easily from First Trinity, Cambridge, and the Eton and Westminster crew from Oxford; but in the Ladies' Plate, the Thames Crew, with Mr. Field instead of Mr. Peacock, were defeated by a quarter of a length. The O.U.B.C. won the Stewards' Cup.——At the Royal Thames Regatta, the Gold Challenge Cup was won by the Thames Club, who beat First Trinity and the Oxford Eton-Westminster crew; First Trinity beat the Oxford University Boat Club and seven other boats for the fours, the winners using a single-strake outrigger. Coombes's crew won the Watermen's four-oared race, and Newell the Sculls

———Westminster beat Eton.———Coombes beat Campbell for the championship, Putney to the Ship at Mortlake.———Newell beat Clasper on the Tyne.

1847. Oxford University beat Cambridge University in the first heat for the Grand Challenge Cub at Henley, and in the final heat the O.U.B.C. beat the Thames Club, the holders. The Visitors' Challenge Cup was established, and was, with the Stewards' Cup, won by Christ Church, Oxford.———At the Royal Thames Regatta the Thames Club beat the Eton (School) Eight for the Gold Challenge Cup; and the St. George's Club won the Amateur Fours. There was no champion prize for watermen's fours.———Eton beat Westminster.———T. and R. Coombes beat R. and H. Clasper, in a pair-oared match, with coxswains, on the Thames, for 100*l.* a side.———Coombes beat Newell for the championship.———Coxswains were abolished in the University pair oars at Oxford.

1848. At the Royal Thames Regatta the Gold Challenge Cup was won by the Thames Club, whose property it then became; and the St. George's Club won the Silver Challenge Cup for four-oars. Clasper's crew won the Champion Fours.———At Henley the O.U.B.C. beat the Thames Club for the Grand Challenge Cup, and Christchurch kept the Stewards' Cup.

1849. Cambridge, who were trained by Coombes, beat Oxford in March, Putney to Mortlake. They had a second match in December, Cambridge coming in first by about half a length, but owing to a foul in Crab Tree Reach, the race was awarded to Oxford, in accordance with Rule IX. of the "Laws of Boat Racing," which had been drawn up by delegates from the two Universities and London a short time previously.——At Henley First Trinity came in ahead of Wadham and Oriel in the race for the Grand Challenge Club, but were disqualified for fouling Wadham, and the race awarded to the latter. The Ladies' Plate was contested by the same three crews, Wadham coming in first, Black Prince next, and Oriel last. The Leander Club won the Stewards' Cup from First Trinity.——At the Royal Thames Regatta there was no Eight-oared race, but the Silver Cup for fours was won by the Thames Club. R. and H. Clasper and T. and R. Coombes, J. Clasper (coxswain), won the Champion Prize for four-oars.——Mr. F. Playford beat Mr. Bone for the Wingfield Sculls on the new course, Putney to Kew.——The Cambridge University Four-oared race was established.

1850. This seems to have been a very bad year for boat racing, the Oxford University Boat Club rowing over for the Grand Challenge and Stewards' Cups at Henley; and Lincoln College, Oxford, for the Ladies' Plate.——At the Thames Regatta, Mr. Knollys says the Silver Challenge Cup for fours was rowed over for by the Oxford University Boat Club, but *Bell's Life* is silent on the subject, merely stating that the Champion Fours were won by Newell, T. Mackinney, R. Doubledee and Coombes, W. Cox (coxswain).

1851. In the race for the Grand Challenge Cup at Henley, there were only two starters, viz., Oxford and Cambridge Universities, and the former won, but Cambridge broke a rowlock soon after starting. Oxford was ahead at the time. Mr. J. W. Chitty, Q.C., rowed stroke of the winning boat. The C.U.B.C.

won the Stewards' Cup.——At the Thames National Regatta for Watermen (as the Putney Regatta was this year called), there was no four-oared race, the competition being limited to pair-oared and sculling races.——Robert Coombes beat Thomas Mackinney for the championship of the Thames.

1852. Oxford beat Cambridge at Putney, Mr. Chitty rowing stroke to the former.——Oxford University were to have rowed over for the Grand Challenge Cup, but at the request of the Stewards raised a second Oxford eight and made a race of it, the winners to be called the O.U.B.C., and the losers the Oxford Aquatic Club. The O.U.B.C. won the Stewards' Cup. The Argonauts Club of London won the Visitors' Cup, this being their first year at Henley.——The Thames Regatta was defunct, and there was but very little boat-racing anywhere, the sport appearing to be temporarily on the wane.——Thomas Cole, of Chelsea, beat R. Coombes for the championship in May, and again in October.——J. Candlish, of Newcastle, beat T. Mackinney on the Thames, and subsequently on the Tyne.

1853. At Henley Regatta the Universities of Oxford and Cambridge were the only competitors for the Grand Challenge Cup. Oxford had the Berkshire station, while Cambridge were outside. The latter had the best of the race as far as Poplar Point, where they led by about 20 feet, but by a rush in the slack water, and as one of the oars of the Cambridge crew was knocked out of its rowlock by a collision with something on the river, Oxford won by 18 inches. The O.U.B.C. won the Stewards' Cup. The umpire's crew was perhaps one of the best watermen's eights ever got together, consisting as it did of T. Mackinney, R. Newell, R. Doubledee, J. Messenger, W. Pocock, J. Phelps, T. Cole, and R. Coombes (stroke).——Messenger beat J. Candlish, of Newcastle, from Putney to Mortlake.

1854. Oxford beat Cambridge from Putney to Mortlake.——First Trinity, Cambridge, won the Grand Challenge Cup and Ladies' Plate, from Wadham College, while Pembroke won the Stewards' Cup.—— The Thames National Regatta for watermen was established at Putney, the champion fours being won by the Elswick crew, Winship, Cook, Davidson, and Bruce, Oliver (coxswain); while a four-oared outrigger, presented by an amateur, was won by the two Mackinneys, Cole, and Coombes, D. Coombes (coxswain). ——There is also a record of Winship, Davidson, Bruce, Maddison, Cook, T. Clasper, Wood, and H. Clasper, of the Tyne, defeating in an eight-oared race at the Thames National Regatta, Kelley, Goodrum, Newell, the two Mackinneys, Cole, and the two Coombes.——J. Messenger beat T. Cole for the championship.——H. Clasper beat Newell from Putney to Mortlake, receiving two lengths start.

1855. The Oxford and Cambridge University crews met at Henley, in the race for the Grand Challenge Cup, there being but one heat, which was won easily by the latter. The Royal Chester Rowing Club won the Stewards' Cup, this being their first appearance at Henley. The Diamond Challenge sculls were won by Mr. A. A. Casamajor—one of the most extraordinary scullers who ever lived—who made his *début* on the occasion. With Mr. Nottidge, rowing as members of the Argonauts Club, he won the Silver Goblets from an Oxford and a Cambridge pair.——Mr. Casamajor also won the Wingfield Sculls, defeating Mr. Herbert H. Playford, the holder, and retained the prize for the unparalleled number of six years. ——The Shakespeare crew, hailing from Manchester, and composed of S. Wood, T. Carroll, H. Ault, and M. Taylor, Maloney (coxswain), won the champion prize at the Thames National Regatta.——Henry Kelley beat J. Mackinney from Putney to Mortlake, the latter capsizing.

CHAPTER XV.

HISTORICAL RECORDS (*continued*), A.D. 1856 TO 1875.

THE Oxford and Cambridge University Boat-race became an annual match in 1856, rowed on the London water at Easter. In this year the crews rowed from Barker's rails above Mortlake to Putney, on the ebb tide, and, after a tremendous struggle all the way, Oxford beat Cambridge by half a length, the boats being alongside nearly all the way.——At Henley the Royal Chester Rowing Club won the Grand Challenge Cup, with great ease, from their only opponents, the Lady Margaret Boat Club, of Cambridge; and the same club also won the Ladies' Plate from the Lady Margaret crew, and Exeter College, Oxford. Up to this time eights had been constructed with keels, but the Chester Club rowed at Henley in the first eight built without a keel, by Matthew Taylor, of Ouseburn, near Newcastle-on-Tyne, who was then working as a shipwright at Birkenhead. This boat was purchased by Exeter College, who in the following year, although they had a very weak crew, went Head of the river, and won the Ladies' Plate at Henley. In this year the London

Rowing Club was established, but, not having been in existence a year, its crews could not compete under its name. Its crack four, composed of Messrs. J. Nottidge, A. A. Casamajor, James Paine, and Herbert H. Playford (stroke), F. Levien (coxswain), rowed as belonging to the Argonauts Club, of which they were members, and won the Stewards' Cup. They also won the newly established four-oared race for the Wyfold Cup, which in 1847, and subsequently, had been awarded to the best of the challengers for the Grand Challenge Cup. Lady Margaret beat the Chester four for the Visitors' Cup, and Mr. Casamajor won the Diamond Sculls for the second time consecutively.——The champion four-oared prize at the Thames National Regatta, was won by a mixed North and South country crew, composed of H. Clasper, and R. Chambers, of the Tyne, and W. Pocock and T. Mackinney of the Thames, G. Driver (coxswain); and the scullers' race, in old fashioned boats, by Robert Chambers (of St. Anthony's) afterwards champion.——Kelley beat J. Mackinney on the Thames, and subsequently Buttle, of Norwich, in two matches on the Yare.

1857. Oxford, rowing stroke on the bow or starboard side, beat Cambridge, from Putney Aqueduct to the Ship at Mortlake. From this time races were started from the Aqueduct instead of Putney old Bridge. Having taken warning from the success of the Chester boat at Henley in the preceding year, the Universities adopted the modern keelless eights, Oxford rowing in a new boat built by M. Taylor, who was with them during their training, and

Cambridge in one by the Salters.——This year witnessed the successful *début* of the London Rowing Club at Henley, in the Grand Challenge Cup, for which there were but two entries, the Oxford University Boat Club, and the L. R. C. The latter had the Berkshire station, and led out at once, drawing clear before reaching Remenham. The Oxford crew then began to overhaul them, but in the bight below Poplar Point the L. R. C. drew away again, and led by a length and a quarter at the grand stand, when No. 4 in the Oxford boat broke his oar, London winning by the distance just mentioned. The Oxford crew were the same that rowed against Cambridge at Putney, but the oarsmen were differently arranged, and in the following order: Messrs. J. T. Thorley, R. W. Risley, R. Martin, H. Wood, E. Warre, A. P. Lonsdale, P. Gurdon, J. Arkell (stroke), F. W. Elers (coxswain); while the London boat was manned by Messrs. J. Ireland, F. Potter, C. Schlotel, J. Nottidge, J. Paine, W. Farrar, A. A. Casamajor, H. H. Playford (stroke), H. Edie (coxswain). Mr. Playford's rowing weight was 9st. 11lb., while of the rest of the crew two were under ten stone, three under eleven, and the rest under twelve. The L. R. C. also won the Stewards' Cup, with the same crew as in 1856, and Mr. Casamajor won the Diamond Sculls for the third time. The Ladies' Plate and Visitors' Cups were now competed for by the clubs of colleges and public schools, instead of being open to rowing clubs in general.——The champion four-oared race at the Thames National Regatta was won by the Newcastle crew, composed of J. H. Clasper, A. Maddison, R. Chambers, and H. Clasper, Short (coxswain). J. H. Clasper (now of Oxford), states that in this race he practised sliding on a fixed seat, though only to a very limited extent, no one else in the crew doing so.——Kelley beat Messenger for the Championship.

1858. Cambridge beat Oxford from Putney to Mortlake, the winners rowing in a boat by M. Taylor, and the losers in one by Searle. This was the race to which Oxford men look back with the greatest dissatisfaction, for whatever chance of success they had —and they believe they would have won—was annihilated by an injury to the rowlock of the stroke oar, which happened immediately after the start, through catching a crab.——Cambridge University beat the Leander Club easily in the trial heat, and also the London Rowing Club in the final heat for the Grand Challenge Cup by nearly half a length, after a punishing race, Cambridge being inside and London outside. London rowed over for the Stewards' Cup, and so did Mr. Casamajor for the Diamond Sculls; Messrs. Playford and Casamajor winning the pairs from Messrs. Warre and Lousdale, of Oxford.——Eton beat Radley in an eight-oared match on the Henley course.——At the Thames National Regatta the champion four was manned by G. Francis, S. Salter, T. White, and G. Hammerton, G. Driver (coxswain).——The Claspers beat the Taylors in a four-oared match on the Tyne; and H. Clasper beat Campbell, a Scotchman, on the Clyde, and subsequently on Loch Lomond; but he was beaten by Thomas White on the Thames.

——J. H. Clasper, of Newcastle, beat G. Francis, of Teddington, Putney to Mortlake.

1859. Oxford beat Cambridge from Putney to Mortlake in very rough water, the Cambridge boat getting waterlogged and sinking under the crew off Barnes, to the dismay of the layers of odds, for a finer crew was said never to have come out of Cambridge.—— The occurrences of this year at Henley will ever be memorable, for it was the good fortune of the London Rowing Club to defeat both the University crews for the Grand Challenge Cup. There were three entries: London, Oxford, and Cambridge. In the trial heat London met Oxford and won by two-thirds of a length; and in the final heat defeated Cambridge. The London crew was composed of Messrs. G. Dunnage, W. Foster, F. Potter, W. Dunnage, W. Farrar, J. Paine, A. A. Casamajor, and H. H. Playford (stroke), H. Weston (coxswain). Since this event no Oxford or Cambridge University crews have entered at Henley; but crews which were to all intents and purposes University crews have competed, and with a great amount of success under such titles as Etonian Club, Radleian Club, Granta Club, Pitt Club, &c. The Stewards' Cup was wrested from the London Rowing Club by Third Trinity, Cambridge, after a terrific race, by nearly 2ft., the Cambridge boat being outside and London inside. The Kingston Rowing Club made their *début* at Henley with a four for the Wyfold Cup, but were unsuccessful.——The champion prize at the Thames National Regatta was won by Clasper's Newcastle crew.——Robert Chambers, of St. Anthony's, beat T. White on the Tyne in the spring, and in the autumn defeated H. Kelley, of Fulham, for the championship of the Thames.——G. Hammerton, of Teddington, beat S. Wright, of Norwich, from Putney to Mortlake.——George Drewitt, of Chelsea, a celebrated landsman, beat Thomas Pocock, of Lambeth, from Putney to Barnes Bridge.

1860. Cambridge beat Oxford from Putney to Mortlake by a length for the last time for ten years.——First Trinity, Cambridge, won the Grand Challenge and Stewards' Cups at Henley, and rowed over for the Ladies' Plate. Mr. H. H. Playford won the Diamond Sculls by a length from Mr. E. D. Brickwood, the holder, after defeating in the trial heat Mr. L. P. Brickwood, of London, by two lengths, and Mr. T. R. Finch, of Oxford, by four lengths.——At the Thames National Regatta the champion fours were won by H. Kelley's crew, Mat. Taylor's crew being second, and Clasper's third.——Eton and Westminster rowed from Putney to Chiswick, this being the first match between them since 1847, and Eton won very easily.——Drewitt, 26 years, beat H. Clasper, 50 years, on the Tyne.—Chambers beat T. White for the championship of the Thames, time 23 min. 15 sec.; and Hammerton beat Drewitt from Putney to Mortlake.

1861. In this year commenced the extraordinary succession of Oxford victories in the University boat race, which continued for nine years, Cambridge coming up year after year only to be defeated. The Oxford crew, which was one of the best ever sent up to Putney— Mr. W. M. Hoare (stroke)—won very easily.——Henley Regatta was notable for the appearance of three eight-oared crews, which had never competed there previously—the Kingston, Eton College and Radley College Boat Clubs—the two latter rowing off their match in one of the heats. First Trinity, Cambridge, won the Grand Challenge Cup, Ladies' Plate, Stewards' Cup, and Visitors' Cup. Mr. Casamajor, once more and for the last time, rowed for the Diamond Sculls, defeating Mr. E. D. Brickwood by two lengths and Mr. George R. Cox by three and a half lengths, the race being rowed off in one heat.——Mr. Casamajor having resigned the Wingfield Sculls, a meeting of past holders was called, and the course shortened—the distance to be from Putney to Mortlake, instead of to Kew: Mr. E. D. Brickwood won them for the first time on the new course.——Messrs. L. P. and E. D. Brickwood won the Corby Castle Challenge Cup for pair oars at the Talkin Tarn Regatta, in Cumberland, for the second year in succession, whereupon it became theirs absolutely: the Naworth Castle Cup for four-oars, being likewise won by the Tyne Amateur Rowing Club, and retained by them.——Eton beat Westminster from Putney to Hammersmith.——The champion fours at the Thames National Regatta were won by an amalgamated crew, consisting of G. Hammerton, J. Tagg, E. Winship, and R. Chambers, R. Clasper (coxswain).——The Sons of the Thames Regatta was established at Putney by Mr. H. H. Playford, and lasted three years, having brought out J. H. Sadler, of Putney.——J. H. Clasper beat T. Pocock twice. —— G. Everson, of Greenwich, beat G. Hammerton.——J. Mackinney beat G. Drewitt.

1862. The London Rowing Club won the Grand Challenge Cup at Henley; University College, Oxford, the Ladies' Plate; and Brasenose the Stewards' and Visitors' Cups. In the Grand Challenge Cup Trinity College, Oxford, beat University College, but in the Ladies' Plate University College turned the tables on Trinity, and beat them cleverly, their stations being reversed. A dead heat was rowed for the Diamond Sculls between Messrs. E. D. Brickwood and W. B. Woodgate, but in rowing it off the former won with great ease.——The Wingfield Sculls for the first time went to Oxford by the success of Mr. Woodgate.—— Eton beat Westminster from Putney to Hammersmith. ——A Challenge Cup for four-oars was established at the Barnes and Mortlake Amateur Regatta, and was first won by the London Rowing Club.——The champion four-oared prize at the Thames National Regatta once more went to Newcastle by the aid of Clasper's crew.——T. Hoare, of Hammersmith, beat E. Eagers, of Chelsea, Putney to Mortlake.

1863. University College, Oxford, won the Grand Challenge Cup, the Ladies' Plate, and the Stewards' Cup, and Brasenose the Visitors' Cup.—— In the Thames National Regatta, G. Hammerton's crew won the champion prize.——R. Chambers beat R. A. Green, of Australia, from Putney to Mortlake; and also G. Everson, of Greenwich.——R. Cooper, of Redheugh-on-Tyne, beat G. Everson.——A scullers' race was rowed at Newcastle for the Tyne champion cup. Considerable fouling occurred between Chambers and Kelley, but the cup was awarded to the former by the umpire.

1864. The Kingston Rowing Club won the Grand Challenge Cup at Henley for the first time on record.

Eton won the Ladies' Plate for the first time in the annals of that prize, beating Trinity Hall, Cambridge, and Radley in the trial heat, and rowing over for the final; University College, Oxford—the holders—withdrawing. The London Rowing Club won the Stewards', and University College, Oxford, the Visitors' Cup.—— Eton beat Westminster for the last time in a match from Chiswick Church to the Star and Garter at Putney.——The champion fours at the Thames National Regatta fell to G. Hammerton's crew.——Chambers and Cooper rowed a match on the Tyne, which, owing to considerable fouling, was re-rowed, when Chambers won.——James Percy beat H. Clasper on the Tyne. ——T. Hoare beat H. Cole from Putney to Mortlake.

1865. The Kingston Rowing Club again won the Grand Challenge Cup; while Third Trinity won the Ladies' Plate, after a great deal of fouling with Eton, as well as the Stewards' and Visitors' Cups.—Mr. E. B. Michell beat Messrs. Lawes and Woodgate for the Diamond Sculls, but Mr. Lawes won the Wingfield Sculls, beating Mr. Michell.——The champion prize at the Thames National Regatta was won by the Sons of the Thames, J. Sadler's crew.—— Chambers beat Cooper on the Tyne, in a mile race. ——J. Sadler, of Putney, beat G. Drewitt, Putney to Mortlake: and T. Hoare, of Hammersmith, beat T. Cannon over the same course; Hoare's time in a pelting rain being 9min. 15sec. to Hammersmith Bridge, and 23min. 15sec. to the Ship.——Kelley beat Chambers for the championship, Chambers sliding on a fixed seat; time 23min. 23sec.——Magdalen beat Caius College at King's Lynn Regatta, though the latter was higher in the College Eights.——A Sweepstake of 50*l*. each, with 100*l*. added, was sculled for on the Ouse, at King's Lynn, between H. Kelley, R. Chambers, and R. Cooper, in which Cooper, after fouling Kelley, came in first by a length, Chambers three lengths astern of Kelley. On appeal from Kelley, the referee disqualified Cooper and awarded the race to the former, the second prize going to Chambers.

1866. The Etonian Club of Oxford won the Grand Challenge Cup; Eton the Ladies' Plate; and University College the Stewards' and Visitors' Cups. The Leander Club sent an eight to Henley, but it was unsuccessful.——The Metropolitan Amateur Regatta was established at Putney, with a Champion Cup for eights, won by the London Rowing Club, a cup for four-oars, won by the same club, and other prizes.——Hammerton's crew won the champion fours at the Thames National Regatta, which after this year became extinct.——J. Sadler beat T. Hoare from Putney to Mortlake.——Chambers beat Sadler for the championship, a foul occurring during the race. Mr. Woodgate rowed Hoare from Hammersmith to Barnes Bridge, and lost by two and half lengths, paying Hoare 10*l*. for rowing him.——H. Kelley beat Hammill, of the United States, in two consecutive days' matches on the Tyne.—J. Percy beat J. H. Clasper; J. Taylor also beat J. H. Clasper, on the Tyne.——J. Taylor beat J. Percy on the Tyne.

1867. In the University match Oxford beat Cambridge by half a length after a tremendous race, neither boat having been clear of the other.—— The Oxford Etonian Club again won the Grand

Challenge Cup; Eton the Ladies' Plate; and University College the Stewards' and Visitors' Cups.——Regattas were held at Paris, one under the management of a French, and the other under an English committee. In the former a professional crew from St. John's, New Brunswick, who rowed without a coxswain, one of the crew steering by his feet, won the four-oared prize from the London Rowing Club, who were second, the Oxford Etonians, who were third, and four Continental crews. In the English Regatta the Eight-oared prize was won by the Old Etonian crew, who beat Corpus Christi College, Oxford, the London Rowing Club, and Worcester College, Oxford; the fours by the Etonians, who beat the London Club and Worcester College; the pairs by Messrs. E. L. Corrie and M. Brown; and the sculls by Mr. W. Stout, of London, Mr. Woodgate being disqualified for fouling. In the Watermen's races the fours were won by the Albion crew of Newcastle, manned by J. Taylor, M. Scott, A. Thompson, R. Chambers of St. Anthony's (ex-champion), T. Richardson (coxswain); the pairs by R. Cook and H. Kelley; and the sculls by Kelley.——Kelley beat Chambers on the Tyne——M. Taylor beat H. Clasper on the Tyne——Sadler beat Cooper on the Thames.——Hammerton beat Drewitt.——A disputed race between Kelley and Sadler ended in a law suit (*Sadler* v. *Smith*), stakes being drawn.——Sadler beat Percy, who slid on a fixed seat, on the Thames, and again at King's Lynn.

1868. The London Rowing Club won the Grand Challenge Cup, defeating, in the final heat, Eton. The latter won the Ladies' Plate from University

College and Pembroke College, Oxford, First Trinity, Cambridge, and St. Peter's, Radley. London also won the Stewards' Cup—Brasenose being disqualified for rowing in a trial heat without a coxswain—and University College the Visitors' Cup. A new race called the Thames Challenge Cup for second class eights was this year established, and won by Pembroke College, Oxford.——The same Newcastle crew which was successful in Paris in 1867, but with Robert Chambers of Wallsend substituted for Robert Chambers of St. Anthony's, won the champion four-oared prize at the new Thames Regatta, which was established on the ashes of the old meeting.—— James Renforth, of Newcastle, won the sculls, as he pleased, from Percy and Sadler, his time from Putney to Mortlake being 23 minutes 15 seconds.——Renforth beat Kelley for the championship of the Thames; and Kelley beat Sadler, also from Putney to Mortlake.

1869. The Oxford Etonian Club won the Grand Challenge Cup again, Eton the Ladies' Plate, the London Rowing Club the Stewards' Cup, and University College, Oxford, the Visitors' Cup. A prize was given for fours without coxswains, for which two crews entered, and was won by the Oxford Radleian Club.——At Henley this year the new plan of apportioning certain weights to the coxswains of eight-oars first came into practice: they had previously always steered at catch weights, but now they were placed on a regulated scale. It was laid down by the committee that coxswains should carry weight according to the average weight of their crews—7st. being the minimum—and the plan has been found to work well. Full particulars of it will be found in Chapter IX.——Oxford beat Harvard (U.S.A.) in a four-oared match with coxswains from Putney to Mortlake, the winning crew being manned by F. Willan, A. C. Yarborough, J. C. Tinné, S. D. Darbishire, J. H. Hall (coxswain).——The champion prize at the Thames Regatta fell to Hammerton's crew; Renforth again winning the Sculls.——J. Taylor and J. Renforth beat A. Thompson and M. Scott, in a pair-oared match on the Tyne.——J. Bright beat Renforth, who gave two length's start, in open boats on the Tyne, through a foul.——J. Sadler rowed over the Putney to Mortlake course to claim the stakes in a match with Walter Brown, the United States Champion, who was unable to start through indisposition.—— The Tyne crew, J. Taylor, T. Winship, J. Martin, J. Renforth, T. Wilson (coxswain), beat the Thames crew, J. Sadler, H. Kelley, W. Messenger, G. Hammerton, R. Hammerton (coxswain), in a four-oared match, Putney to Mortlake.——The same Newcastle crew beat the same London crew differently arranged, Kelley rowing stroke, on the Tyne, a fortnight afterwards, the match having been a home and home one.—— J. Sadler and H. Kelley, however, beat J. Taylor and J. Renforth in a double sculler's match on the Tyne. ——Walter Brown, of America, beat W. Sadler in a match on the Tyne.

1870. Cambridge, with Mr. Goldie, stroke, coached by Mr. G. Morrison, of Balliol College, beat Oxford: this they continued to do until 1875.——Henley Regatta was remarkable for the first appearance on the Thames of the Trinity College Boat Club from Dublin University, who—following the example of the London Rowing Club and Eton—have never missed sending an eight regularly, not by fits and starts, to the regatta, since their first appearance. They rowed in the first heat for the Grand Challenge Cup, but were defeated by Kingston, who won the heat, and the Cambridge Pitt crew. In the second heat the London Rowing Club on the outside beat Eton, after a capital race, by two-thirds of a length. In the final heat on the second day the Oxford Etonians, who were the holders, and who, consequently, stood out from the trial heats, won easily from London. For the Ladies' Plate, Trinity, Dublin, beat Radley in the trial heat, but were defeated by Eton in the final race. The Stewards' Cup was won by the Oxford Etonians by a bare half length from London, after a splendid race, a Lancaster crew being third. Trinity College, Dublin, won the Visitors' Cup, beating the University College crew from Oxford, containing four 'Varsity blues. Eleven eights, fifteen fours, six pairs, and nine scullers went to the post in the two days' racing.——A Newcastle crew, stroked by Robert Chambers of Wallsend, won the champion fours at the Thames National Regatta; J. H. Sadler winning the sculls.——An International four-oared race without coxswains was rowed at Lachine, in Canada, between an English crew from Newcastle-on-Tyne, manned by J. Taylor, T. Winship, J. Martin, and J. Renforth, and the St. John's crew of New Brunswick, manned by G. Price, S. Hutton, E. Ross, and R. Fulton, who rowed as amateurs at Paris in 1867; and in the result the English crew, guided by Taylor, by means of a mechanical apparatus fitted to his stretcher, won very easily. The Newcastle crew slid on fixed seats.——H. Kelley beat J. Bright on the Tyne in open boats—a foul which occurred being awarded to Kelley.——J. H. Sadler beat H. Kelley in a match from Putney to Mortlake.——J. Taylor beat J. Percy on the Tyne.

1871. At Henley the Oxford Etonian Club won the Grand Challenge Cup; Pembroke College won the Ladies' Plate by rather more than half a length from Eton—Trinity, Dublin, being third and last in the final heat. London won the Stewards' Cup from the Kingston and Oxford Etonian Clubs in the deciding heat; and First Trinity, Cambridge, won the Visitors' Cup from Trinity, Dublin. This was another monster regatta at Henley.——The champion fours at the Thames Regatta, were won by Calderhead's crew from Glasgow. The sculls were no longer open, but were confined to competitors who had only rowed for limited sums of money.——Renforth and Kelley beat J. Taylor and T. Winship in a pair oared match on the Tyne, in January.——A four oared match for 500*l.* aside, without coxswains, was rowed on the Kennebeccasis River, in New Brunswick, between an English crew and the St. John's four, and will ever be memorable as the contest which caused Renforth's death. The English crew was composed of J. Percy, R. Chambers of Wallsend, H. Kelley, and J. Renforth, and the St. John's crew were the same as in 1870. The Tyne crew led for a quarter of a mile, when it became evident that something ailed Renforth, as he swayed from side to side in the boat; shortly afterwards his oar dropped from his hand

and he fell back into the arms of Kelley, who rowed No. 3; upon this Percy and Chambers pulled the boat ashore, and in an hour Renforth died. The St. John's crew, therefore, finished the race alone.—— This four next refused to compete against the two English crews which rowed at the Halifax regatta a week later, and though entered, withdrew. At this regatta a four-oared prize of 600*l.* was won by J. Taylor, R. Bagnall, J. H. Sadler, and T. Winship; a Halifax crew (Pryor's) second; Percy, J. Bright, Kelley and Chambers, of Wallsend, third; the Biglin-Coulter crew, of the United States, fourth; and two other Halifax crews fifth and sixth. Chambers' crew took a long lead but went a wrong course, so Winship won. The scullers' race for 100*l.* was won by J. H. Sadler, who beat G. Brown of Halifax (2), H. Kelley (3), R. Bagnall (4), H. Coulter, U.S. champion (5), and Lovett, of Halifax (6).——At Saratoga Regatta held in the United States soon afterwards, the Cornwall-on-Hudson crew of the four Wards won the first prize for fours, beating the crew of Chambers of Wallsend (2) Winship's crew, †; and the Biglin-Coulter crew, †; the Poughkeepsie, and the Pittsburg crews. Biglin's and Winship's crews led nearly to the turning buoys, where they went out of their course, the Wards' and Chambers' passing them. In trying to overtake them Biglin's and Winship's crews fouled, and lost their chance whatever it might have been—the Wards' winning by four lengths, Chambers one length ahead of Winship, and Biglin, who rowed a dead heat for third place. The prizes were—first 400*l.*, second 250*l.*, third

150*l.* Sadler won the first prize of 200*l.* for scullers, and Kelley the second of 100*l.*, J. Biglin of the U.S. third, E. Ward fourth, Bagnall and Bright fifth and sixth.——A regatta was also held at Longeuil, in Canada, at which Chambers' and Winship's crews met a Nova Scotian crew (Barton's). The two English fours soon left the local four astern, but at the turning buoys went the wrong course, by which the Halifax crew got in front, and the Englishmen were unable to catch them. Kelley won the sculler's prize. ——Quebec Regatta succeeded, and Chambers' crew won the 100*l.* prize for four-oars from five other crews who were non-professionals, but entered to make a race: their names were not to be obtained, possibly for fear of being disqualified as amateurs. Kelley won the sculls, beating Chambers of Wallsend, and Percy.——On their return to England, a match was made and rowed on the Tyne, between Winship's and Chambers' crews, and was won by the former, entirely through using the movable seat, which they had seen the Biglin-Coulter crew rowing with at the Halifax and Saratoga Regattas above-mentioned, and which Taylor fitted to his boat for the match. Chambers' crew rowed on fixed seats. Henceforth the introduction of the sliding seat became general.

1872. An International four-oared match, in boats without coxswains, was rowed on the ebb tide from Mortlake to Putney in June—though it was intended to be rowed up—between a London Rowing Club crew, composed of Messrs. John B. Close, F. S. Gulston (who steered), A. de L. Long, and W. Stout, and a crew of the Atalanta Boat Club, of New York, the former winning from end to end. The London boat was fitted with the new sliding seats, but the crew was so superior that the fact of the Americans using fixed seats in no degree affected the result.—— The London Rowing Club won the Grand Challenge Cup and the Stewards' Cup at Henley, while Jesus College, Cambridge, won the Ladies' Plate, and Pembroke College, Oxford, the Visitors' Cup. In one of the trial heats for the Diamond Sculls, in which Messrs. C. C. Knollys, of Oxford, and J. H. D. Goldie, of Cambridge, met, a foul occurred, the heat being awarded to Knollys, who spurted and touched his opponent while out of his own water, but Goldie came in first. The final heat was won by Knollys. In this year the holders of prizes competed in the trial heats on equal terms with challengers, instead of standing out and rowing in the final heat only, as before. Presentation prizes for non-coxswain fours, offered with the view of inducing the Atalanta crew to compete at Henley, were rowed over for by the London Rowing Club crew, who beat the American crew at Putney, the latter withdrawing. One of their number, however, competed for the Diamond Sculls, but after winning one trial heat, was defeated. The London Rowing Club's eight and other boats, were all fitted with sliding seats, which perhaps contributed to their successes, as they had practised on them before reaching Henley. After their arrival on the scene of action the Pembroke College, Kingston, and other crews, set to work to have the new seats fitted to their boats, but though done at the eleventh hour, the advantage was most marked. Some crews rowed on sliding and some on fixed seats, but all the scullers used slides.——The champion fours at the Thames Regatta fell to a Hammersmith crew, stroked by W. Biffen, jun.

1873. The London Rowing Club again won the Grand Challenge Cup at Henley, and also the Stewards' Cup, in the race for which non-coxswain fours were used for the first time. Jesus College, Cambridge, repeated their victory of 1872 in the Ladies' Plate; and the Trinity College, Dublin, four won the Visitors' Cup.——Biffen's crew again won the champion fours at the Thames Regatta.——Kelley beat James Taylor on the Tyne.——R. Bagnall beat Kelley.

1874. The Grand Challenge Cup for the third year, and the Stewards' Cup for the fourth year, consecutively, went to the London Rowing Club: First Trinity, Cambridge, won the Ladies' Plate by little more than half a length from Trinity, Dublin, and previously found some difficulty in shaking off Eton in a trial heat. Trinity, Dublin, won the Visitors' Cup for the third time, and second year in succession.——Biffen's crew for the third time won the four oar'd prize at the Thames Regatta.——Sadler beat Bagnall for the championship on the Putney course in the spring.——W. Lumsden and R. Boyd, of Newcastle, beat T. Green and H. Thomas, of London, in a double scullers' match on the Tyne; and, later on, Lumsden and Boyd beat Winship and Bagnall in pair oars.——G. Brown beat E. Morris for the championship of North America on the Kennebeccasis river.

1875. Oxford beat Cambridge very easily.——The Leander Club for the first time since 1840 won the Grand Challenge Cup. Trinity College, Dublin, also attained the object for which they had striven since their first appearance in 1870, and won the Ladies' Plate for eight-oars. London won the Steward's Cup, and University College, Oxford, the Visitors' Cup from Trinity College, Dublin. In the pair-oared race for Silver Goblets, Messrs. A. de L. Long and F. S. Gulston, who had won three times previously, were by far the best pair, and had paddled in front of their opponents, but easing too much in rounding Poplar Point, and being bumped while out of their proper water by Messrs. Chillingworth and Herbert, were disqualified, and the cups awarded to the latter.——Mr. A. C. Dicker, of Cambridge, won the Diamond Sculls for the third year in succession, defeating, among other competitors, Mr. F. L. Playford, of London, who subsequently turned the tables on him by winning the Wingfield Sculls at Putney, which Mr. Dicker had held for the two previous years.——The Champion fours at the Thames Regatta were won by a Newcastle crew.——Bagnall beat Lumsden at Newcastle; and R. Boyd beat Sadler on a mile course on the Tyne.——Sadler, however, beat Boyd on the Thames for the championship.——J. Higgins beat A. Strong, Putney to Mortlake: time, 23min. 9sec., fastest on record.

N.B.—The Putney to Mortlake course has been rowed by Oxford in 20min. 5sec. on fixed, and by Cambridge in 19min. 35sec. on sliding seats.——The Henley course has been rowed by eights in 7min. 18sec.

PART II.—TRAINING.

CHAPTER XVI.

Its Principles.

THE moral and physical man is connected closely and intimately, and if health, strength, and longevity are to be secured, it is of absolute importance that whilst the mind is cultured and refined, an equal attention should be paid to the training and education of the creature. With the body in health, the muscles in full and vigorous action, the mind is far better able to grapple with and overcome the more difficult problems of intellectual philosophy. To those who never reflect, "to eat, drink, and sleep," seem all that is necessary to prolong and sustain existence, but man both thinks and acts. The brain, whence flow thought, reflection, mind, requires culture, and the human frame, the most perfect of all machines, with its muscles, bones, and sinews, must be educated. The brain overtasked reacts upon the body, producing mal-assimilation, with its train of evils, indigestion, hypochondriasis, low spirits, and impaired vital energy.

The overtasked body equally, though perhaps not so rapidly, produces the same results. This being admittedly true in regard to the ordinary conditions of existence, is doubly so as affecting boat-racing—a class of contest which taxes the powers and endurance of the human frame to the very utmost. It is indispensable, therefore, that every man who takes part in these competitions, should undergo a careful and gradual process of preparation to which the term "training" is applied. By "training" I mean the physical amelioration of the oarsman as opposed to his scientific education—the improvement of the bodily powers, not the inculcation of the principles and correct form of rowing, which has already been dealt with.

Training, then, is the art of attaining physical excellence, by which a man is enabled to meet extreme and exceptional demands upon his energies, without permanent injury to his powers or system. To acquire this excellence of condition, exemplified in increased strength and muscle, improved wind, and accelerated speed, it is necessary to submit to the immediate influence of all the agents whose office it is to promote bodily health and strength; in order that when the hour of trial comes he may perform his allotted task of putting forth all his forces without flagging, without distress—and, indeed, with comparative ease. On the other hand, it has been urged that men have been injured, and their lives shortened, by the severe training they have been made to undergo; but whether it be true or untrue in regard to a time long past, it is more than doubtful if such is the case now—training

ITS PRINCIPLES. 199

being far better understood than it was formerly, and being, moreover, conducted on rational principles, where all was empiricism.

The agents of health consist of exercise, diet, sleep, air, bathing, and clothing. How these agents are to be employed so as to produce the best results, next claims attention.

First. Exercise of the whole frame is more conducive to health than that of particular limbs. It induces perspiration, and thereby removes noxious matters—consequently it aids in the purification of the blood; and it stimulates the several functions of the body. It tends to the proper destruction of the tissues, the removal of worn out, and the hastening forward of fresh, material for its replacement. Of all exercises, perhaps, none is more calculated to give general tone to the system than that of rowing; at the same time that the wish to excel, stimulated by the prestige which accompanies such excellence, imparts vigour and strength to the mind. In doing this it attains three distinct results: it increases the size and power of the voluntary muscles employed; it augments the functional capacity of the involuntary muscles; and it promotes the health and strength of the whole body by increasing respiration and quickening the general circulation. This being the nature, and these the results, of exercise, it is imposed upon a man in training for a boat-race, in two forms:—first, rowing; second, running or walking—in the one case training for strength, in the other training for wind. Now, rowing promotes the acquisition of muscular power by giving employment to the arms, the back, the loins, the hips, and more than all, to the legs, especially since the introduction of sliding seats. It promotes the acquisition of good wind, particularly in spare men, but it is advisable to have recourse to a certain amount of walking or running in all cases; but more especially in dealing with men of full habit and fleshy. Pedestrianism not only acts beneficially upon the legs and loins, but it is invaluable for improving the wind. It must be borne in mind that to a man of full stature, from sixteen to twenty respirations per minute are the normal rate, while a racing stroke is from thirty-six to forty per minute, and as the breathing is to a great extent regulated by the stroke, the rate of respiration is increased from sixteen or twenty to thirty-six or forty. The heart, too, in rowing a race contracts about one hundred and ten times instead of seventy-five times a minute. Hence the necessity for improving the respiratory powers, and hence also the reason of the well-nigh killing effect of rowing at racing pace when unprepared. And something more than long-continued and careful preparation—that is to say, sound internal organs are required to enable a man to continue his actions, and to withstand the awful feeling which comes over him, during the distressing interval between the going of the first and the coming of the second wind: this being more especially exhausting to a sculler, who has no opportunity of easing himself, be it ever so little, at the expense of his companions—as he can in an eight—till the sensation passes away.

Secondly. Diet comes next in importance. Exercise creates a want which it is the place of food to supply. Now food may roughly be divided into two

ITS PRINCIPLES.

kinds: First, that which is principally applied to the formation of flesh or tissue; secondly, that which is applied to the production of heat. In cold countries or weather fatty or heat-producing food is requisite; but in hot climates, and in summer, a diet mainly of a farinaceous and leguminous nature is found to be preferable, and the mode of life being, as a rule, less active than in cold climates, flesh forming food is not so necessary. It is sufficient for the purposes of these chapters, that in this country a considerable proportion of animal combined with a due admixture of farinaceous and vegetable food is the best; for variety of food is a dictate of nature. Quantity is regulated by the appetite. The times for refection are well known to be at intervals of from four to five hours: the precise hours are immaterial, as they must depend upon occupation and the most suitable times for practice. Regulation is essential. Stated meals should be taken at stated times. Food should be eaten slowly and masticated well. Drink also should be taken slowly and not too often. *A man should never eat what he knows will disagree with him.* As hunger is the warning voice of nature telling us that our bodies are in need of a fresh supply of food, so thirst is the same voice warning us that a fresh supply of liquid is required. Thirst, then, being, like hunger, a natural demand, may safely be gratified, and with water in preference to any other fluid. The prohibition often put upon the use of water, or fluids, in training may often be carried too far. To limit a man to a pint or two of liquid per day when his system is throwing off three or four times that quantity through the medium of the ordinary secretions, is as unreasonable as to keep him on half rations. The general thirst experienced by the whole system consequent upon great bodily exertion or extreme external heat, has but one means of cure—drink, in the simplest form attainable. Local thirst, usually limited to the mucous linings of the mouth and throat, may be allayed by rinsing the mouth and gargling the throat, sucking the stone of stone-fruit, or a pebble, by which to excite the glands in the affected part; or even by dipping the hands into cold water. Drink is here of very little benefit, as the fluid passes at once to the stomach, and affords no relief to the parts affected; but after rinsing the mouth, small quantities may be swallowed slowly.—— The field for the selection of food to meet the wants of the body under every condition of physical exertion is by no means restricted. All that the exceptional requirements of training call for, is to make a judicious selection; but in recognising this principle, rowing men have formed a code of dietary composed almost wholly of restrictions, the effect of which has has been to produce a sameness in diet which has almost been as injurious in some cases, as the entire absence of any laws would be in others.

Thirdly. Sleep is equally necessary to rest the body and to refresh the mind. The amount of time required for this purpose varies not only with individuals, but with the same individual at different periods of life. It is influenced by various causes, by the action of the other agents of health, and especially by exercise. The growing and immature frame requires a much longer time for recuperation than is necessary at a later period of life, when growth and development are virtually complete. In the latter case there is but one day's wear to restore, whereas in the former there is a permanent and continuous demand for the body's enlargement and consolidation. Hence, youth requires the most, and middle age the least sleep,— the want increasing again in old age. Eight hours are customarily named as the standard amount of sleep required under ordinary circumstances by an adult in fair health, and although seven hours may sometimes be found ample, eight will be better.

Fourthly. The importance of fresh air is generally understood and admitted, but is by no means so universally acted on. Much could be said on the very imperfect ventilation of bedrooms. A man in training should have at all times pure air, and plenty of it; and if his throat and lungs are sound he may sleep with his window partially open, but great care must be exercised in this respect in cold weather, and when the wind is in the east. Care should also be taken that a draught does not blow over the body, as it will rapidly lower its temperature, and a cold will result. Early rising is always to be commended, for nothing is so exhilarating as the sensation experienced in going out into the fresh invigorating morning air—say at Henley, in June.

Fifthly. Bathing must be viewed as an agent of health in two distinct aspects; first in its capacity as a cleanser of the skin, next as an agent of considerable tonic power. In its first aspect it addresses the skin as the organ of perspiration only, with the view of removing from it all impediments to functional ability, and arousing it to greater activity; in the second, as the organ of sensation, possessed of great nervous sensibility and influence, acting directly through it on the nervous and circulatory systems. With the first object in view, the use of tepid or lukewarm water and soap every three or four days, at such times as may be convenient, will not be inopportune, or, according to modern fashion, an occasional Turkish bath, though perhaps not when in strict training. In view of the second object, a cold tub in the bedroom should be taken every morning immediately on rising, and may be again resorted to on return from practice, and if sea salt can be thrown into it so much the better. Many a man prefers a plunge into the sea where attainable, or into the river. To this there is no objection whatever, provided only he does not stop in. Neither a cold nor a warm bath should be taken within several hours after a meal.

Sixthly. Clothing is another important agent, for the evaporation of heat and moisture from the surface of the body is impeded, not only by the number of garments worn, but by their shape and size, the closeness of their texture, and the nature of the material of which they are made. Thus linen is more obstructive to the evaporation of moisture than cotton, and cotton than woollens. For rowing, therefore, the lightest woollen or mixed woollen and cotton garments should be worn. They should consist of merino jerseys of a moderately thin texture; one or two thick knitted woollen jerseys to wear over the thinner ones when practising in cold weather, or to put on when getting out of the boat; a flannel or pilot-cloth boating-coat warmly lined (according to the season), in which it is as well to have a band of elastic round the wrists to prevent the wind blowing up the arms in cold, windy weather; flannel caps, woollen comforters, straw hats, flannel trousers, and thin white shoes—which are perhaps best made of canvas, and which can be pipe-clayed when dirty—worn over ordinary woollen socks. The inside of the seat of the trousers may be lined with a large soft skin of washleather to prevent the fibres of the material irritating the cuticle; but it is of course entirely optional. It has the disadvantage, if much worn, of getting hard after becoming wet from perspiration, or from water coming in over the side of the boat. Great care should be exercised in getting the boating jacket or over-jersey properly made. Tailors, it should be remembered, seldom or never build a good one. It ought to be lined with flannel, as it is often put on immediately over the rowing jersey.

CHAPTER XVII.

Its Practice.

WE now come to the application of these principles to the daily life of the oarsmen in training, which is the province of the trainer.

The trainer is a highly important personage, and exercises an all-powerful influence on his crew, either for good or for evil. His duties are of a varied character, and many of them are exceedingly simple; but at the same time a minute technical knowledge, which can only be gained by long experience, is absolutely requisite. Amongst other things, it will be part of his duty to select the best men from a number of oarsmen placed at his disposal; to reduce to the actual number necessary for manning the boat the lot originally selected, and to assign to each his proper thwart, after repeated trials; to be their constant companion both indoors and out of doors; to regulate their hours of work, leisure, and repast; to order and preside at their meals, exercising a strict supervision over everything, and practising as much as possible what he preaches. His text should be: Never ask a man to do anything you won't do yourself. He should be careful that his men run into no excess, and that they do not break through the rules laid down for their guidance, excepting in so far as he may permit in peculiar cases. He should watch over them as far as practicable in their hours of idleness, although it generally happens that much is unavoidably left to their own honour and discretion; nevertheless, no one who has any regard to the object in view, or to integrity of principle, will abuse the confidence thus necessarily reposed in him. He should keep his men in good humour, and in perfect accord with one another and themselves—for it is better to have a bad oar than a bad-tempered man in a crew — studying their various constitutions and tempers, smoothing down and making easy any little disagreements and want of patience that may arise on account of the severity of their treatment, by pointing out the temporary nature of the hardships which they are undergoing, and by calling their attention to the great and glorious result to be achieved. He should at all times lend a willing ear to complaints, either as to oars and the mechanical portions of the boat, or to incipient symptoms of training off, weakness, or other bodily ailments, giving them an attentive and careful consideration; and should any of his men exhibit signs of going amiss, it should be his endeavour, by a slight relaxation of work, and by permitting a somewhat more free indulgence in the matter of diet, as he may think best, in the exercise of the great discretion left to him, to prevent bad becoming worse. In fact, he should always encourage his men to tell him of the slightest thing that is wrong with them, reticence in this respect being probably the greatest difficulty he will have to contend with; for, be it recollected, it is much easier to train a man down than it is to put on condition once lost. He should accompany the crew in their walks and runs, directing them like a skilful general; and he should be particularly strict and attentive when they are in their boat. He must take care that they can get at their work properly, that it is neither too near nor too far off; that their seats are of the proper height, and that all the little technicalities of oars, buttons, rowlocks, slides, stretchers, &c., are correct in every detail. He must watch and instruct them from the banks of the river as well as from the stern of the boat (especially the former), pointing out their faults, suggesting remedies, and correcting errors; and in order to do this he must thoroughly study each individual oarsman in his crew, and find out the cause of his faults—no such easy task as it appears, as it differs in each individual, and is usually quite different from what it seemed to be at first sight. He must see that they do not over-exert themselves; but he must likewise take care that they undergo sufficient work, and that there is no shirking, and yet that the willing horses do not bear all the labour. He should occasionally cheer the whole crew when doing well, and likewise encourage particular men if they deserve it, holding them up to the least careful and painstaking, as models to be followed; but he should repress untimely efforts on the part of individuals. He must reprove offenders, temperately but firmly, and always insist on being obeyed. He should be competent not only to detect the slightest fault or tendency to error, but to show how to remedy it for the nonce, and to guard against it for the future. He should know exactly the proper amount of work to be done, and the manner in which it ought to be done. He should be able to distinguish the signs and appearances of men being underworked or overworked, and should guard against their going amiss. He should be a first rate judge of time, form, and pace, as well as of condition. Now, judging condition is perhaps the most difficult thing a trainer has to do, because men, from pride and fear of being turned out of the boat—from too much pluck, in fact—will not tell him if they are ill. Hence, many of the evil consequences of rowing, sure to do damage to the individual himself after the race is over, and likely to lead to the most troublesome of all things as far as the crew are concerned—defeat. In this especially it is as well to take the advice of some old rowing man—a trainer if possible—who sees the crew at long intervals, as the changes from good condition to training off are very slight, and are apt to escape the observation of one who sees it every day. This refers more particularly to individuals, as it is not very difficult to tell if a whole boat is going wrong. The trainer should be able to tell at a glance whether men are thriving or falling off under the regimen he is enforcing, and to single out those who have been doing their best from those who have been sparing themselves during a hard pull. To sum up, he must be an accomplished and thoroughly practical oarsman, possessing an accurate knowledge of rowing and training in all its details; and this can only be acquired by a long apprenticeship at the oar, and by a minute and critical observation of the style and form of every one afloat. Finally, he should be concise yet withal intelligible, perfectly audible, vigilant, impartial, good-tempered, and considerate.

The men to be trained necessarily vary much in physical characteristics. Some have been living a different life from others—this one steadily, that one fast. One is tall and heavy; another gaunt, thin, and wiry; a third of middle height, broad shoulders, and sturdy build. It is, therefore, self-evident that they will require treatment more or less diversified. It is, however, sufficient for the present purpose to assume that none are positively out of health or without practice; such an event is, or ought to be, rare; for no one who has any regard for his future well-being and who does not positively desire to injure his constitution, will subject himself to the hardships of a course of strict training unless he is sound and free from disease. It would, in fact, be a good plan if every man who was selected for a crew, were to undergo a careful medical examination, and so learn whether he would be running a risk in submitting to be put to very severe work. At any rate he would have the satisfaction of knowing that he was not doing wrong; for it is scarcely to be supposed that, if forbidden by his medical adviser, he would still continue to follow the bent of his own inclination, however mortifying it might be to be debarred from forming one of the crew. The individuals who, after repeated changes and alterations, have been finally determined upon, must make up their minds to devote themselves to the object in view, and to spare no pains to render themselves perfect. They must do their work willingly, however unpalatable it may prove, and not shirk. They should obey their trainer in all his orders, and comply readily with his instructions, recollecting that he is advising and admonishing them for their own improvement and benefit. They should work and submit with a will and with a good grace, not sullenly or in ill-humour. They should always confide in their Mentor, and should not hesitate to make him acquainted with all their little grievances of whatever nature, in order that he may suggest a remedy—not maintaining an obstinate or dogged silence, nor brooding over imaginary wrongs and hardships. If they find themselves getting overdone or distressed, they should speak, in order that one stitch may save the otherwise inevitable nine. They should not neglect ordinary precautions against cold, such as taking a comforter and jacket, or over-jersey out with them in the boat ready for stoppages, &c., or to occupy their spare moments with light and agreeable reading, or some other innocent diversion; and they should be careful to avoid dwelling upon the probable chances of defeat, or worrying themselves as the anxiously expected day approaches.

The time occupied in getting a crew properly fit will, in a great measure, depend upon the season of the year, weather, length of course, and other concomitant circumstances; but, generally speaking, from three to six weeks will be requisite from first making up till they are ready to go to the post.

The men should all be weighed at the commencement of training, and subsequently not less often than once a week during practice.

One point must not be passed over without notice:

the custom which obtains in some quarters or is recommended in some systems of training, of physicking the crew all round. If a man is in a fair state of health, sufficient to warrant his going into training, the presumption is that he does not need drugs; if unwell, he had better go and consult his own medical attendant.

The general health of the men should be improved by the ordinary precautions of regular and early hours, bathing, walking, and rowing; by eschewing smoke, drink, and ill-ventilated or heated rooms; by abstaining from excesses of every description, *e.g.*, by keeping their bodies in temperance, soberness, and chastity—the motto of a trainer; by relaxation from literary or sedentary occupation as much as possible; by amusing the mind and elevating the spirits; by moderation in all things, and by the strictest regularity of habit: the system must be invigorated by good sound food and refreshing rest; and, above all things, it is necessary that the men trained should enter heart and soul into the task before them.

They should rise in spring between seven and eight o'clock; in summer from half-past six to half-past seven, but they should have at least eight hours' sleep clear, or perhaps even more in some cases. The bath may follow immediately, if taken indoors, or even if bathing in the open air is resorted to; still, it is optional, and perhaps better to get through the morning walk of a mile or two first, and to bathe afterwards. It usually happens that the bathing-place is some little way off the crew's head-quarters, and therefore the walk home is sufficient to produce a comfortable glow; if it is close at hand, a brisk walk of half a mile should intervene between the bath and the morning meal. There should be *no running before breakfast.*

The time of breaking fast should be an hour or an hour and a half after getting out of bed, though there can be no objection to the consumption of a piece of stale bread or a hard biscuit, with a glass of water or milk, the first thing after rising. From breakfast to half-past twelve or one o'clock is the period for work, or study, as before mentioned, and a smart walk or a run of a mile if particularly required to reduce fat will not be improper. The mid-day meal will either be a moderately light dinner, or generally speaking, lunch. At the appointed hour the crew will get into their boat for a hard row, which will vary from five to ten miles, as explained in the first part of this book. After returning from the row, and on getting out of the boat, some pedestrianism may be had recourse to if considered necessary; and here the trainer will, according to his judgment, require some to run, others perhaps to walk only. Walking at a smart pace, as a rule, will not alone reduce fat, though in some cases it may, and therefore recourse must be had to running. A sharp run of a mile, or even less, is far better than a dull, steady drag of four or five miles, which will depress the spirits, and tire the body; for it must be borne in mind that the race to be gone through is not a running, but a rowing match, and therefore plenty of rowing, as opposed to much running, is to be desired. Having arrived at home, the hot and wet flannels should be taken off, and the skin rubbed dry with a rough towel—letting this be a thoroughly brisk rub, and not merely a formal wipe-down. After rowing, the men should not be long in turning the boat, getting out of her, going indoors and stripping, if they do not run. They may then wash as much as they like, in tepid or in cold water, with or without sea salt, at their option, and don a fresh change of clothing. This will bring them up to meal time. After dinner the spare hours may be passed in light reading and rest, even in a semi-recumbent posture, but sleep is forbidden.

A far greater latitude is admissible in the matter of diet than is generally allowed, and the more varied the repast the more gratefully will it be accepted. Nothing is so sickening as to be for ever sitting down to chop, stale bread, and tea, varied only by steak, stale bread, and beer; and no one will thrive on such a bill of fare for a week, still less for a month or more. The meals should be taken at the same hour every day, and no stone should be left unturned to make the time spent in refreshing the inner man as genial and agreeable as possible. It cannot for an instant be imagined that it is better to sit down and silently gobble up one's daily rations, with the certainty of indigestion following upon bolted morsels, than to spend a reasonable period in properly masticating one's food—the while enlivened by agreeable conversation—and in allowing it to digest. As to articles of diet, everyone knows, or ought to know, what suits him best, and what does not; and short of allowing anything positively injurious or unwholesome to be put on the table, too much consideration cannot be shown to men's inclinations; for it should not be forgotten that what is one man's food is another man's poison. The author of the "Principles of Rowing and Steering," well observes: "Whatever a man's habits have been, if reasonable and temperate, let him merely modify them now, upon general sanitary principles; and let him not be converted, just four weeks before a race, into an artificial creature, feeding only on the most flesh-forming food, dreading the innocent adjuncts of everyone's table in ordinary life, and trusting to beef and mutton and strong ale to deliver him."

Breakfast should consist of broiled meat, such as mutton chops, rumpsteaks (if tender), or occasionally cold meat, tea, and bread, or toast and butter. To these may be added some cold chicken, or hot grilled fowl—not too highly seasoned—an egg or two, if it agrees with the individual taking it, and lettuce or watercress. Brown bread is useful as well as white. The meat should be well cooked—just done to a turn, as it is commonly called, not blue or half raw—but yet full of gravy and the natural juices; the bread, it is perhaps unnecessary to say, should invariably be stale. Two cups of tea may be taken; it should not be drunk too hot, or too strong. Salt and pepper may be used to make things tasty. Porridge need not be discontinued if it has been the custom to take it, but it is not an article that should be specially introduced upon the training table. For lunch, a slice or two of bread and butter and a glass of beer or sherry; but for a man in strong work such food is insufficient—it will be better to take a slice of cold meat, or a chop, and bread, together with half a pint of good sound ale or a little wine if used to it.

Dinner is the most important meal in the day. Its chief foundations are beef and mutton, either in the form of roast sirloins and ribs of beef or rumpsteaks, or of roast legs, loins, haunches, or saddles of mutton, and mutton chops, with here and there a boiled leg for the sake of variety. To these may be added roasted or boiled fowls, game, venison, &c. The use of lamb is good, but salted meats are forbidden, and veal and pork are better eschewed. It may appear strange, but the ancient Greek athletes were accustomed to live a great deal on pork, which seems to have been to them what beef and mutton are to us. Veal was also used by the great prize-fighters sixty years ago, for they were continually having small meals of stewed veal, boiled chickens, and sherry. Though not advocating their use, all this tends to confirm the idea that temperance, soberness, and chastity are the main points, and that little rules, such as whether watercresses are good or bad, are unimportant. A bit of fish may frequently be given with advantage, such as cod, turbot, brill, or sole, but it should be boiled. Plenty of stale bread, as well as a due allowance of vegetables, is indispensable. The latter include potatoes, cauliflower, brocoli, young greens, spinach. and French beans. A pint of sound beer will be the proper quantity, though it may now and then be increased to a pint and a half in summer, but not if the dinner precedes the rowing. A light pudding is also welcome: it may be varied by an occasional dish of plain cooked fruit. The great thing is to give the men sufficient solid food; but as the most vigorous appetite cannot be always enjoying simple meat and bread, it is proper to vary the dinner, day after day, with other dishes. Bread and butter, with watercresses or a lettuce, may conclude the meal, but pulled bread crisply baked is far more palatable than the crumb of an ordinary loaf. After dinner a couple of glasses of claret, sherry, or port wine, may be given to each man, accompanied by some hard dry biscuits, and perhaps a jelly, or an orange or two. About nine o'clock the last meal—which is truly only an apology for one—should be ready. It may consist of a cup of tea and a slice of bread, but a pint of watergruel with some dry toast is far better, though all men cannot stand it, as, if insisted on, it is prone to lead to sleepnessness. Where nourishment is much needed a glass of warm liquid jelly may be substituted. Strictness will apply to regular hours and careful ways more than to the exact articles of food set before the crew, as has already been said. Indeed, it would be preferable to vary the diet still more. The following observations on the training of the Oxford crew of 1858, by Mr. Edmond Warre, then President, is extracted from the O.U.B.C. book :—"The training which the crew went through was, perhaps, the most perfect in system that has ever been acted upon. The consequence was that not one of the crew ever suffered from the usual weakness from boils, which in most cases torment men in training. . . . . The dinners were at the Cross, and the diet was the usual beef and mutton, varied occasionally with fish and poultry, and there was always a plain pudding of rice, sago, or tapioca afterwards. To this system must be attributed the good health of the crew."——The tendency of men in training is to suffer periodical returns of weakness about every seven or ten days, principally because they are kept in too high condition, and are worked too hard. A moderate amount of exercise, combined with a strictly regular life, ought to be sufficient to keep men in good health without an extraordinary amount of running, and without turning them into beef and mutton eating animals. Every possible variety in the way of fish, fowl, and pudding ought to be allowed them. If they do look rather fat a week before the race, it ought to be a subject of congratulation, as the trainer can easily bring them down, and has all the more chance of putting finish on them, because he can make them work more at the critical period—in short, he has his crew better in hand. Again, on a long course it is usually strength, not the perfection of wind, that decides the race, for the stroke is slower than on a short one, so that it is better to be a little undertrained, with strength, than overtrained with wind.

Appetite will fix the limit of food at the various meals, and therefore it is as well to allow every one to suit his own inclination. If thirst is frequent, the best remedy is a small draught of cold spring water, though it should not be drunk by anyone in a state of perspiration; but dipping the hands and washing in cold water help almost as effectually as anything to quench it. An occasional and gentle stroll during the spare time in the day will not fail to be of advantage; but men must not be suffered to lounge about, as it takes a great deal out of them. Standing about looking at games and sports generally results in staleness in the back and loins next day.

The final week of practice is generally spent on the course on which the boat-race is to be rowed, the crew removing thither from their ordinary *locale;* but no alteration in work, of any consequence, will be advisable until the last day or two, as the crew will require sending along on their new arena, as much to put the finishing touches on their rowing as to accustom them to the strange water. One good hard row a day is ample, but if it is deferred till the evening, a steady paddle for a mile and a half out and back, or three miles in all, in the forenoon, will not be improper if it be not too hot. No severe work should be done during the last two days, as the strength should be allowed, as it were, to gather itself up for the final effort: this time will be far more profitably spent in practising rapid starts, as in the actual race itself—starts, say, from a dozen strokes to a couple of hundred yards.

On the day of the match an ample meal of roast mutton, with bread and half a pint of beer, should be set before the men two or three hours previously to starting, unless the race comes off within a reasonable time after any regular repast—say three hours. If too long a period intervenes, and yet not sufficient for a full meal, a crust of stale bread or a hard biscuit may be eaten, accompanied by a little pale brandy and cold water. The quantity may be a wineglassful, of one third or one half brandy, filled up with water. Some men cannot avoid becoming nervous—to a greater or less extent—as the eventful moment approaches, and I know of nothing that acts more suitably than the above, although Dutch courage is highly objectionable. If the race is rowed in heats, with only a brief interval between them, a glass of warm port-wine negus and a morsel of dry biscuit, or a cup of tea without milk or sugar, but with a teaspoonful of brandy in it, will be beneficially partaken of.

It is assumed that each individual has now been educated according to nature, common sense, and the correct principles of the trainer's art. When brought out to perform his long-expected task, his strength is gathered up, his fully developed muscles are hard as iron, his wind is sound, his tread elastic, his speed great, his flesh firm, his skin fair and clear, his face hard and healthy, though perhaps fine-drawn, his eye bright and sparkling like a diamond—the white a clear blue—and his spirits, accompanied by a proper confidence in his ability to go anywhere and do anything, of the very best.

These are the essentials of perfect condition and of success.

CHAPTER XVIII.

PROHIBITIONS, AILMENTS, ACCIDENTS, &c.

AMONG things which should not be done, the following may be enumerated. In the first place, absorbing intellectual labour and sedentary occupation should as much as possible be laid aside, and all mental excitement or anxiety should be avoided. The hour of rising should not be too early or unreasonable, and no violent exercise which will cause profuse perspiration should be taken before breakfast, as the system is thereby weakened. Hard rows and long runs at an early hour are especially to be deprecated; they cause lassitude, loss of appetite, and a feeling of general debility and staleness throughout the day.

In bathing, caution is very necessary, for serious consequences are often produced by suddenly entering the water in a state of profuse perspiration. At the same time, the body should be quite warm; therefore, a brisk walk to the bathing-place is highly desirable. Of course, it is prejudicial to stop in the water too long; a couple of plunges and a short swim intervening between them will be the correct thing. After rowing hard, great circumspection is requisite to prevent a cold being caught; men, therefore, should never stand about after getting out of their boat, but should put on warm coats, tie up their throats, and, unless they run, go indoors as quickly as possible, to have a rub down and to change clothes. Draughts of cold water or of other cold liquids should never be taken while in a heated state. Before sitting down to meals the men should always rest for a short space, and also for some time after them. No sleep is permitted after dinner or tea, until the proper hour of bedtime arrives. Violent exercise should on no account be taken immediately after a heavy meal, for to this cause may to a great extent be attributed the premature decease of a celebrated sculler some years since. Fresh air in the sleeping apartments is essential, as ill-ventilated rooms are unhealthy; and if the men can bear their windows partially opened (weather, of course, permitting) without catching cold or sore-throats, so much the better, supposing their rooms are not sufficiently ventilated otherwise. Standing about on wet ground or on dewy evenings should be guarded against, and so should lying down on the grass in warm weather, because the more powerful the sun, the greater the evaporation, and the chances of an attack of rheumatism. Exposure to the rays of the sun in summer is injurious, and particularly so on the day of the race. If it is absolutely necessary to go out of doors, it is a good plan to carry an umbrella to protect the head and neck. The rowing clothes should always be well dried before being again used.

Numerous articles are inadmissible in training diet, but much depends upon the constitution of individuals.

However, all things which bear the ordinary reputation of being highly indigestible, should be eschewed—such as the majority of raw vegetables, and, in some cases, eggs, if they prove constipating, which they frequently do. The same may be said of much toasted bread, and for the same reason: no green tea should be drunk—black tea, not too strongly infused, is the best. It should, however, never be taken very hot. Coffee is best avoided. Cocoa is not so objectionable, but it does not agree equally well with everyone. White butchers' meat, such as veal and pork, all salted flesh, and highly seasoned dishes, are better untouched. As previously mentioned, there is no harm in using the ordinary condiments—such as pepper, salt, and mustard, or even ginger—as they promote digestion; they should not, of course, be taken to excess. Radishes, cucumber, celery, horseradish, onions, pickles, &c., must be shunned; so likewise must pastry, tarts, and such-like rubbish. Soups are not allowed, neither is cheese, nor much raw fruit, although the more wholesome kind of fruit is very beneficial. At dinner, and sometimes at lunch, beer of some sort is the rule—indeed, some men do better with beer than with sherry at lunch. The chief kinds to be guarded against are those that are bottled, also washy bitter beer, which is in general use on ordinary occasions, and very old ale. The last-mentioned is, however, a great favourite with many trainers, and especially with those of the old school, but it is apt to make men slightly inebriated. Nothing can be better for our purpose than the magnificent ales which are drawn in some of the colleges at our Universities—if not too strong—or the best Burton. When wine is given after dinner, it should not be mixed. The crew should confine themselves to one description, and it should never be succeeded, in the same evening, by gruel made with milk. Dried fruits after dinner are best dispensed with, if I except figs.

The last and the most important thing to be forbidden is tobacco. Practice has proved that it is better to prohibit smoking during training than to permit it; it is consequently condemned. Still, it is perhaps an open question whether in very exceptional cases it may not be allowed—say, for instance, when a man has been in the habit of smoking a great deal, and has to work hard with his brain in the evening. One smoke before going to bed would not do much harm, and might conduce to sleep, sometimes difficult to get under the circumstances.

Amongst the most common errors which occur during the preparations for a race is the use of physic. At the commencement of training a little may be required in some very exceptional cases, when it is better to apply to a medical man. Another mistake often committed is that of taking violent exercise early in the morning, as above mentioned. Some trainers are in the habit of putting their men through too much work in the day. Not content with one long row in the course of the twenty-four hours, they set them to hard work in the morning, and then to run one or two miles. In the evening, after returning from their customary practice afloat, they are sometimes sent out again on a second trying cruise, *e.g.*, taken out of their eight and set to row two or three miles at their best speed in a four, till nature is quite exhausted. No wonder if, after two or three weeks of such handling, they come to the post pallid, overtrained, and weak. Monotony of diet is another source of evil. The fact of sitting down to the same articles of food, meal after meal, and day after day, will upset the appetite of the most voracious. This also should be carefully provided against, especially as the list from which to make a selection is in itself at best excessively limited. So, also, the prevalent custom of withholding a proper proportion of vegetable diet during the day cannot be too strongly condemned. Too great a severity likewise is sometimes exercised in restricting drink, and in preventing the relief of parching thirst.

Various unforeseen evils frequently occur during practice, and though many of them are beyond measure trivial in themselves, yet they cause much discomfort and annoyance. They comprise staleness or training off, blisters, boils, &c., &c. When they appear, the only thing is to cure them; but it is far wiser to guard against them by taking thought beforehand than to treat with indifference what may possibly lead to defeat.

The chief and most important is training off, or going amiss. It cannot always be prevented, but by care and vigilance on the part of the trainer it may be checked on the first symptom. It generally makes its unwelcome appearance in consequence of too hard work, more particularly if the weather is hot and oppressive. Sometimes it may be caused by too constant a repetition of the same diet. In the first case a rest from work for a day or two will set matters right, but occasionally it should be accompanied by a change of air for the same period—such as a removal to the seaboard—an alteration to a more generous diet not being omitted. In the second case the variation of food just mentioned will usually suffice, but a slight relaxation of work as well will produce the desired result more speedily.

Blisters are of universal occurrence, especially at the commencement of the season, when the hands are soft from their long rest during the winter: but with a man accustomed to rowing they are usually a sign that he does not hold his oar tight—a bad fault, as it leads to many others. The feet are also sometimes troubled with blisters, but in this case they arise from walking, not from rowing, and are comparatively speaking rare. Nevertheless, after a little practice and judicious treatment, the hands soon become hard and callous, and their worst feature is their somewhat unsightly appearance. Some men find a rough oar suit them best, and they consequently take care to rasp the handle well; others, on the contrary, prefer it smooth, and scrape it with glass, rubbing it smooth with sand paper afterwards. The best course to take when about to commence racing practice, is to prepare the hands gradually for the work they have to undergo. For this purpose some steady paddling will prove most serviceable; the palms of the hands may also be rubbed with salt and water, or with brandy, to harden them. If, nevertheless, blisters arise, they must be done away with as quickly as possible. To effect this, some people pursue one plan, some another. If the little bladders have not burst, they are not much trouble; a needle with a piece of worsted may be run through them, and the worsted be left in; or they can be pricked with a clean needle, and the water squeezed out carefully, the aperture being made as small as possible, and in an oblique direction, where there is likely to be least pressure or friction. Notwithstanding this, the outer skin will often peel off, and the inner and tender cuticle be exposed. There are many opponents of this plan, and possibly they are right, for the reason just given. It is far better to dissipate the water, and then the skin reassumes its former position, but by that time it has become hardened and callous, and ceases any longer to be troublesome. To effect this, after washing, when the row is completed, take spirit of camphor and rub over the bladders, letting the spirit evaporate by waving the hand in the air; this process should be repeated frequently, and they will disappear. But when the blister unfortunately bursts during a pull, and the contact of the air and the friction of the oar aggravate the inflammation, a very sore place is sometimes created, and is proportionately difficult to heal. Care should be taken to prevent grit or dirt getting into the wound, and cotton wool may be applied under an old kid glove. The gloves should not be white kids, as they often cause great irritation, being, I believe, dressed with poison. Entire rest from taking an oar will soon be followed by a rapid cure, but it usually happens that this is impossible, and that the oarsman's services cannot be spared for a single day. Under these circumstances, after every particle of dirt has been removed, the wound should be dressed either with plain grease—such as pure tallow, spermaceti ointment, or zinc ointment. Glycerine is sometimes recommended, but, though very healing, it causes excessive pain when applied. The zinc and other ointment mentioned may be obtained from any chemist. Over the grease some finely carded wool, or a piece of soft wash leather, may be placed—the former is best—and then an old and easy glove should be put on over all.

Excoriations occur from the friction or galling of the trousers, and usually come from not sitting still on the seat. The best thing to obviate this most uncomfortable ill is to have the rowing trousers or drawers lined with a large soft skin of washleather. Care should at the same time be taken that the leather does not become hardened. Many men rub the inside of their boating trousers with soap before putting them on, and swear by the process as preventing excoriation; oiling them with neatsfoot oil has a similar effect. Should they unfortunately occur, notwithstanding these precautions, they must be treated in a similar manner to those on the hands. A day's rest and bathing in cold water will also be most advantageous.

Boils are an effort of Nature to get rid of a dead piece of cellular membrane by means of inflammatory action. In consequence of some peculiar condition of the blood, of the exact nature of which little is known, a death (or sloughing, as it is called) of a portion of cellular membrane takes place close under the true skin; to remove this foreign body nature sets up an inflammation, which is invariably of a slow and congestive character. It appears as if the poisonous nature of the slough irritates the surrounding parts to such a degree as in some measure to interfere with the process of absorption, and consequently, a painful and hardened circle of swelled and reddened skin is formed around the dead cell. In most cases the thickening is so great as to stop the circulation in the interior of the circle, and the boil remains stationary for a long time. They appear singly or in groups, generally the latter; and I have known as many as twenty or thirty of various sizes upon the same person. They are exceedingly troublesome and painful, and cause also great irritability of temper. They should never be neglected by the trainer; there is no fear of the men affected forgetting them, though they sometimes conceal them. Sameness of diet will very often produce them; but if a due proportion of vegetables be daily administered, and the food be varied as much as possible, there is not so much chance of their supervening. The only remedy for this condition is either the application of some stimulating greasy application, such as a linseed poultice, or division by means of the knife. Either of these remedies more or less puts an end to the inactive condition, and then a healthy suppuration goes on to remove the cell, and by throwing up fresh granulations, as they are called, to restore what has been removed. Such is the nature and ordinary treatment of a boil; but in training it is almost impossible to bear the use of the knife, if the boil is on any part which is subjected to much friction. In other situations it may be used, but when a boil occurs, if the knife is used, at least a week or ten days must be lost before the patient can expose the raw surface to the friction of the thwart. Here, therefore, the best plan is to apply a plaster, spread on leather and composed of equal parts of mercurial and opiate plaster. This stimulates and relaxes the inflamed vessels, and the opiate relieves the pain to a great degree, but even this is only a partial remedy, as without rest it is impossible entirely to relieve boils. To those who are known to be the subject of boils, "Stonehenge" recommends, as a preventive, the use of a wash of nitrate of silver of the strength of 15 or 20 grains to the ounce. This should be painted over the part every night, and will, of course, turn it more or less black, but it seems to give tone to the vessels, and to prevent that low and congestive state which precedes the death of the cellular membrane; at all events it prevents the formation of boils. Benefit may likewise result from bathing the part with bay-salt and water. A tablespoonful of ordinary beer yeast in a tumbler of cold water twice a day, after meals, though an old woman's remedy, is as good and effectual a remedy as any, although exceedingly simple—I speak from practical experience on the point.

Acute rheumatism is quite incompatible with training, and its treatment need not therefore enter into our present inquiry. Chronic rheumatism, on the other hand, is constantly interfering with severe work, and its attacks are anxiously to be avoided. It may be divided into muscular rheumatism and the rheumatism of joints; the former shows itself by the occurrence of pain, often very severe, on the slightest movement, or attempt at movement even, of the particular muscle or muscles attacked, which again are generally quite free from pain while quiescent. On pressing upon the muscles attacked great pain and soreness occur, and the seat of the disease may, in this way, generally be discovered; on the other hand, when in the ligaments around the joints, it requires the joint itself to be moved, either actively or passively, before pain is experienced. Thus, supposing there to be rheumatism of the arm, if the upper and lower arms are firmly grasped so as to fix the elbow, and the patient is told to attempt to bend the elbow, if muscular rheumatism is present he will give himself even more pain than usual; but if the joint only is affected, no pain, or much less than usual, will be felt. During training, whenever rheumatism is so severe as to require interna medicine, the disease is of such a nature as to demand rest, but it often happens that local remedies will suffice, and this is particularly the case with muscular rheumatism. It is generally in those muscles which are more particularly called into play by the nature of the exercise that rheumatism shows itself, and every time exercise is taken, the rheumatic condition only goes off during use, to return with increased activity after a rest. In all these cases prevention is better than cure, and all unnecessary exposure of the body should be avoided, especially if in cold or wet weather. Flannel should be worn next the skin during the day, and after stripping, for rowing or running, the coat should be put on again without delay. As a local remedy, one of the following may be tried, and I give them in the order of their severity, beginning with the most mild. First, take of tincture of capsicum, ½oz.; spirits of camphor, 1oz.; tincture of arnica, 1 drachm. Mix. On using it, add an equal quantity of hot brandy, and rub the part affected for a quarter of an hour. Secondly, take of liquor ammoniæ, spirits of turpentine, laudanum, and neatsfoot oil, equal parts; mix, and rub in before a good fire twice a day. These remedies will often allay any muscular rheumatism which may occur in training, and I have even known rheumatism when attacking the joints subside on the use of the last mentioned application. As I before said, more severe remedies are incompatible with training.

Strained or ruptured muscles occur in walking, and more especially in running. One or more small fibres of the muscular tissue are occasionally overstrained or absolutely ruptured. If the mischief is extensive, nothing but rest will allow of union and reparation, but very slight injuries may be rendered so bearable as to allow of exercise without prohibitory pain, by means of counter-irritants rubbed in externally, and local pressure applied by means of a bandage. The object of the latter is to throw injured muscles "out of gear," to use an engineer's term, and thus enable other muscles to do their work, and to some extent that peculiar to the injured ones, which they could not otherwise do without calling upon the latter to act at the same time. As a counter-irritant nothing is better than a mixture of turpentine, ammonia, and soap liniment, in equal proportions. The bandage requires some skill for its proper application, but not necessarily the hand of a surgeon. It is generally only at the seat of injury, and very often an india-rubber band will act better than any unyielding bandage, however well applied.

Sprain of tendon or joint generally requires more time for repair than sprain of a muscle, as the vitality of these parts is low. If recent, cold applications, such as vinegar and water, with the addition of some spirit, is the best remedy. When the heat consequent on the injury ceases, apply the embrocation recommended for strained muscle, and in a few days have the joints strapped up with brown soap plaster. These injuries, however, are generally so severe as to necessitate recourse to a surgeon. In chronic cases there is nothing like pumping on the part once or twice a day, for a longer or shorter time.

Corns on the feet are not caused by rowing, but result from the pressure of boot or shoe. There are many plans of curing them, but the majority are ineffectual after a certain lapse of time. A removal of the cause of pressure will alone obviate the evil: the shoes should therefore be cut according to the shape of the feet.

Chapped hands are common in cold weather, and rowers are sometimes terribly annoyed as their wrists chap, often to such a degree as to cause them to bleed. For this ailment there is no remedy to be compared with glycerine, which should be freely smeared over the whole surface which is chapped, by means of a brush or feather. The application should be made night and morning.

Hæmorrhoids, hernia, strains in the groin, colds, sore-throats, and other ailments, occasionally obtrude their unwelcome presence, but they should always be submitted to a properly qualified medical man.

I cannot conclude without alluding to a very common but yet most unwise course of procedure pursued by many men when, their race being over, they are out of the hands of their trainer. The gun which proclaims the winning boat frequently appears the signal to break loose and run riot in every conceivable manner; and crews which have for weeks exhibited the most exemplary patience, and have scrupulously adhered and submitted to the rules and regimen laid down for them, indulge in every possible excess. This, and not orthodox training, is the real cause of ill effects afterwards.

APPENDIX.

RULES FOR BETTING.

1. In all bets there must be a possibility to win when the bet is made; "you cannot win when you cannot lose."

2. The person who bets the odds has a right to choose a boat or the field; when a boat is chosen, the field is what starts against it.

3. A bet cannot be off except by mutual consent, but either party may demand stakes to be made on the day of the race—giving reasonable notice thereof—and, on refusal, may declare such bet off.

4. The interests of the bets are inseparable from the interests of the stakes or prize, or, in other words, bets go with the stakes; but bets specially made "first past the post," or "in their places," are determined by the order of passing the post.

5. Bets on boat-races are not "play or pay," with the exceptions hereinafter mentioned.

6. Bets are determined when a boat does not start, *if* the words "absolutely row or pay," or "play or pay," are made use when making the bet.

7. When boats are ordered to take their places for the start, all bets respecting such boats are "play or pay."

8. All double-event bets are "play or pay."

9. If a match or race be made for any particular day in any week, and the day is changed to any other in the same week, all bets stand; but if the day is changed, or the race postponed to any day in a different week, or if the slightest difference is made in the terms of the engagement, all bets made before the alteration are void.

10. If two boats row a dead heat, and agree to divide the stakes or plate, all bets between such boats, or between either of them and the field, must be settled by the money being put together and divided between the parties concerned, in the same proportion as the stakes or plate; and if a bet be made on one of the boats that rowed the dead heat against a beaten boat, the person who backed the boat that rowed the dead heat wins half his bet if his boat receives half the prize; but if the dead heat be the first event of a double bet, the bet is void unless the boat received above a moiety of the prize, which would constitute it a winner in a double event.

11. Bets on boats disqualified before the race are void, under Rule 5.

12. In the event of a draw, all bets are void.

13. Bets become void by the death of either party making them.

INDEX.

Accidents	page 232
Ailments	225
Air, fresh	203
Amateurs, American definition of	132
,, definition of	133
,, qualification of	128
Arrow Rowing Club	136
Atalanta-London Race	193
Babcock, Mr., invention of	27
Backing	55
Bathing	203, 221
Beginners, to teach	78
Betting, rules for	235
Blisters	226
Boat clubs	135
,, hints for forming	140
,, history of	136
,, rules for	142
Boatracing, American laws of	126
,, commencement of	3, 147
,, laws of	116
,, various modes of	102
Boils	228
Breast races	102
Bumping races	103
Cambridge and Leander Club, first match	160
,, and Oxford, first match	154
,, early rowing at	153
,, University Boat Club founded	138

INDEX.

Chapped hands	*page* 233
Clasper's invention	12
Clothing	204
Coaching beginners	84
,, for races	88
Committees, duties of	106
Corns	233
Coxswain, duties of	67
,, scale of weights for	112, 188
Cup, Grand Challenge	164
Daily routine of training	212
Dead heats	110
Description of racing boats	14
Diamond Sculls established	170
Diet	200, 214
Dimensions of racing boats	24, 25
Doggett's Coat and Badge	147
Drinking cold water	201
Easing	54
Eight-oar, stroke on bowside	178
Eight-oar without keel, first	177
Eton and Westminster, first match	154
Eton College Boat Club founded	137
Eton, early rowing at	152
Evils of work before breakfast	221
Exercise	199
Faults generally	62
Faults of labour	60
,, position and form	59
First outrigger	12, 170
Foot steering gear	24
Grand Challenge Cup established	164
Handicap races	105
Harvard-Oxford race	189

INDEX.

Heat of the sun, to be avoided	page 222
Henley Regatta established	163
Historical records	147
Holding water	55
Judge, the	108
Junior, definition of	133
Ladies' Challenge Plate established	170
Laws of boatracing	116
Leander Club, establishment of	136
„ and Cambridge first race	160
London-Atalanta race	193
London, early racing in	147
London Rowing Club founded	139, 177
Muscles, rupture of	232
„ strain of	232
Non-coxswain fours	20, 193, 194
Oars and sculls	23
Officers of regattas	107
Old fashioned wager boats	19
Outriggers, first invented	11, 170
Oxford and Cambridge, first match	154
Oxford, early rowing at	150
Oxford-Harvard race	189
Oxford University Boat Club founded	138
Paddling	54
Pair-oared rowing	99
Prizes, kinds of	109
Professional rowing, decline of	6
Prohibitions	221
Qualifications of amateurs	128
„ rules of Henley Regatta	131

INDEX.

Race-courses, principal	page 114
Races, breast	102
,, bumping	103
,, handicap	105
,, time	104
Racing boats	10
Records, historical	147
Regattas	106, 110
,, establishment of	163
,, Henley, rules of	111
,, officers of	107
Renforth, death of	191
Rheumatism	230
Rowing explained	40
Rowing clubs, hints for forming	140
,, ,, rules for	142
Rudders	23
Rule of the road	75
Running	199, 213
Sculling	56, 85
Selection of crews	88
Seven-oar race, the	168
Shark Rowing Club, date of	136
Silver Goblets established	171
Sleep	202
Slides	14
Sliding on fixed seats	38, 180, 185, 187, 191
Sliding seat	26
,, diagram of	36
,, experiments with	31
,, introduction of	193, 194
,, invention of	27
,, theory of	31
Sprains	233
Star Rowing Club, date of	136
Stewards' Cup established	167
Steering	66
,, at Henley	73

INDEX. 241

Steering in a cross wind	page 71
,, Putney to Mortlake	72
,, mechanical	23, 74
,, round corner	70
Strained muscles	232
Teaching beginners	78
Temple Boat Club	138
Thames Challenge Cup established	188
Thirst	201
Time races	104
Times, quick	185, 188, 196
Trainer, the	206
Training, its principles	197
,, its practice	206
Training off	225
Twelve oars	18
Umpire, the	107
,, appeal to	122
Visitors' Challenge Cup established	172
Watermanship, want of	65
Weighing	211
Westminster College Boat Club founded	137
Westminster, early rowing at	148
Westminster and Eton first match	154
Wingfield Sculls established	156
Wyfold Cup established	178

www.ingramcontent.com/pod-product-compliance
Lightning Source LLC
Chambersburg PA
CBHW021805230426
43669CB00008B/642